Judo for Women

Judo for Women

ROY INMAN, 6th Dan
with Nicolas Soames

The Crowood Press

First published in 1987 by
The Crowood Press
Ramsbury
Wiltshire SN8 2HE

British Library Cataloguing in Publication Data

Inman, Roy
Judo for women.
1. Judo
I. Title II. Soames, Nicolas
796.8'152 GV1114

ISBN 1 85223 040 1

Picture Credits

Line illustrations by Lesley Sayer
Photographs by David Finch

Typeset by Acorn Bookwork, Salisbury, Wiltshire
Printed in Great Britain by Butler & Tanner Ltd, Frome and London

To my wife Carol, who not only supported me during my own competitive years, but whose patience and understanding made a valuable yet unsung contribution to the emergence of a generation of outstanding British women competitors.

Contents

Acknowledgements

No two people worked harder in the initial stages of this book than Ann Hughes and Diane Bell, both being experienced competitors and World Champions, who submitted themselves to arduous video sessions which formed the basis of the illustrations. It is Ann Hughes who shows what an able competitor can do in terms of self-defence. John O'Brian of the High Wycombe Judo Club and Centre of Excellence must also be thanked for his technical video expertise, and Granada TV Rentals (St Albans) for favourable video renting terms. Other thanks go to Richard Bowen and Bill Gilbert for the loan of historical books from their judo libraries.

I must also acknowledge the members of the British women's squads over the years who, in the early days, were subjected to some experimentation and who always responded positively and with alertness. Without realising it, they were laying the foundations for a revolution in women's judo in Great Britain, and perhaps throughout the world.

Preface

A year passed between the time this book was conceived and the time it was written. During that period I noticed significant developments in women's judo, both at grass-roots level of club judo, and in top international competition. The careful attention paid by women to increasing strength and fitness factors is making a surprising impact on the range of techniques that can be done. Slowly, techniques such as *Osoto-gari*, *Uchimata* and even *Uranage* are becoming real possibilities. In essence, the fitter and stronger women become, the fewer will be the differences between men's and women's judo.

It will still be a long time, though, before these changes occur in a major way in clubs, and it will always be necessary for instructors and women judoka themselves to be aware of the differences. I hope this book goes some way to easing the entry of women into the rich study of judo.

Roy Inman
August 1986

Loretta Doyle, 1982 World Champion.

1 Women and Judo

WOMEN IN SPORT

The role of women is very clear in both amateur and professional sports. With a few exceptions, such as mixed doubles in tennis or equestrian events, women compete separately from men and maintain their own level of achievement which is not compared with the achievements of their male counterparts. The times are indeed slower than those of the men, but a world record is in no sense regarded as a lesser attainment, for a women's race is different from a men's race and a women's high jump record different from a men's high jump record. This applies equally to training methods. In training, women are not expected to pit their strengths and match their times against men, but carry out programmes which are often different in order to take into account their different physiques.

All this is easily recognised in those areas of sport where women have competed side by side with men for decades. The combat sports, however, have always presented a difficulty, starting with the reluctance of a male-dominated Western society to admit that women have a part to play in the fighting arts. It has always been acceptable for men to batter each other in a boxing ring or to wrestle in leotards, but it is considered undignified for women to follow suit.

In fact, judo has been responsible for leading a major revolution in the way society sees women and the combat sports, and its acceptance as a demonstration sport in the 1988 Olympics and full status on the Olympic calendar from 1992 has a much broader significance than being merely an additional event.

There is wry irony in this, because judo evolved in a society where women were traditionally accorded an extremely submissive role – at least in the public view. Even in the latter half of the twentieth century, Japan remains the leading industrial nation with the least awareness and acceptance of equal rights for women. Although women were taught judo from the very early days in Japan, for decades their activity was almost totally restricted to Kata, with only the men allowed to enjoy free-fighting randori.

The wider development of women's judo was a Western phenomenon: from the earliest days of judo in the West, women practised with men in normal club training sessions where it was rapidly discovered that women and men were simply too absorbed by the intricacies of judo technique to be overly concerned about assaults on female dignity occasioned by the intimate contact that is sometimes unavoidable. Again, it was the West that developed national and international competition for women, and forced Japan to reconsider its view of female judo.

JUDO TRAINING FOR WOMEN

Despite the fact that women have been competing on an organised international basis for over two decades, and that women form a substantial part of the total judo membership the world over, the role of women in judo, at least at grass-roots level, remains confused.

As a direct consequence, the training of women throughout the world is lamentably unclear, largely because lingering in the minds of most men – and many women for that matter – is the traditional view that size should not affect the efficacy of judo techniques. Judo was established on the basis that the smaller man can overturn the larger man with a deft application of technique, and if this is the case, why should the smaller woman not overturn the larger man?

There is a certain amount of truth in this. A small, skilled woman can undoubtedly throw a hefty man and probably armlock or strangle him into the bargain, but only if there is a major discrepancy in the level of skills. This applies equally to a smaller man against a larger man – a fact which can be seen in the way the leviathans of judo have come to dominate the open weight category competitions. However, the myth of a woman touching the proverbial pressure point and incapacitating a muscled giant is exactly that – a myth, and one that has seriously hampered the development of women's judo as a modern combat sport in the second half of the twentieth century.

As judo grew in popularity in the post-war period, eventually gaining recognition as an Olympic sport for men, pressure began for similar recognition for women. After all, many of the major Western judo countries, such as France, Austria, West Germany, the USA and Great Britain, could point to extremely capable female judoka and a large female judo membership.

Yet not only the male judoka, but the vast bulk of the female exponents and even the leading fighters were unsure of training practices for women. Should the basic physical training for women be different from those well-tried programmes for men? Should the techniques themselves vary for women? Should women simply not consider the use of certain techniques which, however well established as main scoring techniques for men, are just not applicable to women? These questions were not even being asked until relatively recently, and the answers were often based more on good luck than on judgement or even experience.

To find the answers it was not possible to follow the traditional route of consulting the Japanese experience, for clearly that was limited. It was also not possible to investigate other top judo nations such as the USSR, because, for different reasons, women's judo was equally undeveloped there. So every country was left to its own devices to develop women's judo as it saw fit. For the first few years of women's international competition most coaches were men who simply did not appreciate that any difference existed between men's and women's judo. Where women did appear in judo books (generally as a sop to the female membership) they just demonstrated the judo techniques in exactly the same manner as they would be executed by men.

It is only now, as women's judo is on the threshold of the Olympics and can look back to four World Championships, that it is becoming more widely accepted that there is a significant difference between men's and women's judo, due to differences not just in strength factors but other natural attributes. The assumption that women practising with other women equalled men practising with men seemed logical, but was simply not true. In short, on the judo mat women are not men in white T-shirts. For years they have suffered by being forced to do techniques which are incompatible with their physical and mental characteristics, and the fact that they have survived in judo long enough to develop their own style is a tribute both to themselves and to the flexibility and absorbing interest of judo itself.

Evolving a New Attitude

My involvement with women's judo began with the invitation in 1975 to teach the British women's squad one weekend. By the mid-1970s I was coming to the end of my competing career, but there was no indication on that first weekend that I would end up helping to evolve a new attitude towards women's judo, because, like most men, it didn't occur to me that female judo would be any different or would require a complete rethink of established attitudes. All I saw was that the women showed immense enthusiasm, but generally demonstrated a low level of fitness and an even lower level of judo technique. Their basic movements lacked the smooth flow that is the hallmark of the advanced judoka and their throwing and groundwork skills were limited. They had little idea of when to attack and often seemed to end up attacking their opponents' strong points, largely because of ill-considered timing; they also had little awareness of combination techniques.

This is, of course, a generalisation, for within that squad were a few important exceptions, notably Jane Bridge who was to become Britain's first World Champion and Christine Child who was Britain's first European Champion. I only realised some years later that in many ways those exceptions had emerged in spite of the system, not because of it. Women's judo in Britain – and elsewhere – was so much behind the advances made in the men's section because women were treated as weaker imitations of men.

On that first weekend, and for many years afterwards, I continued to treat women on the mat in that way. I taught my techniques, those that had worked for me in numerous internationals, in Japan and in hundreds of domestic competitions, as well as in randori. Some of these techniques are simply not applicable to women, and even those techniques that have been adopted by women over the years, such as certain combinations, have had to be slightly altered in order to make them work in the different environment.

The first Women's European Championships were held in Munich in 1975, when Christine Child won the heavyweight category for Britain, and a year later I became manager of the British Women's Team. The British women continued to make an impression on the medal tables of the few international tournaments that existed – Jane Bridge won her first European title in 1976 – but that was largely because of their natural talent and the fact that Britain possessed a relatively large women's section in the sport. It also reflected the initiative taken by Britain in developing women's international competitive judo.

For the first three years I trained the women in a style which was largely the same as that used by men. I would concentrate on throws and combinations involving *Harai-goshi*, *Uchimata* and *Osoto-gari*, which were the throws I myself used in combination. After a year I realised that something was not quite right because sixty per cent of the squad still couldn't use the techniques in competition, so I started to rethink my approach.

I spent the next two years learning about lightweight judo – the techniques that worked where speed, movement and surprise were the essential elements, rather than setting up the opponent and exploding into a throw with full power. In this I was aided by the enthusiasm of the women themselves; I rapidly discovered that women are more easily 'coachable' than men: if you give them a programme, most follow it religiously.

After those two years of lightweight judo certain ideas were beginning to emerge; this was none too soon for the first World Championships were scheduled to be held in New York in 1980. Those ideas were not sudden realisations, but rather principles that began to establish themselves in most of the work that was being done.

Precision and Fitness

It seems logical to think that while women will appear the weaker sex when matched against men, against other women, especially women of their own weight, there should be no difference. What emerged in those early years was that men, in the execution of a throw, can call on upper body power; men can hit a hard, defensive body and sometimes, with slight adjustment, can complete the throw with sheer strength. Women, however, do not have access to this kind of power; if they attack when the timing and posture are not correct they just collapse. They do not have the power to compensate for mistakes. This is the famed 'flop and drop' judo that was regarded as a hallmark of so much women's judo and junior judo of the time and both for the same reasons. It was very easy for men to criticise, because they did not have to be so precise in their judo as they could power their way out of trouble.

It became increasingly clear that women had to compensate for this lack of power by aiming for greater precision, which meant a greater awareness of when to attack; and they also had to acquire the level of fitness which would allow them to spend much of the contest on the move.

The static, eyeball to eyeball contest of strength and tactics ending in a sudden explosion by one fighter, which is so often seen in top men's judo is largely inappropriate in women's judo – except, perhaps, in the heavier weight categories. Movement was the key. If women could learn to get themselves into position for a throw during the middle of general movement then the chances of the opponent blocking the throw were more limited. They would, in essence, be caught unawares and, moving weight being lighter than dead weight, the chances of a satisfying ippon were that much higher.

It was one thing to realise these basic principles and quite another to put them into practice. Once again, entrenched ideas on training had to be brushed aside and a completely fresh look taken. Fitness sessions and judo training not only needed to be rethought, but experiments in other areas had to be tested.

A major breakthrough, curiously, came with the introduction of music in the warming-up sessions and the *Uchikomi*. The normal 90-minute or two-hour judo practice benefits from the quiet yet purposeful atmosphere which is characteristic of dojos all over the world, but a 20-hour squad session over the weekend was a different matter. It was necessary to find some way of relieving the boredom that often creeps into these long and tiring affairs, and I put together a large number of tapes with the latest pop music – generally loud and rhythmic – which we played at a sensible but considerable volume. It had an immediate effect in that it provided a more relaxed atmosphere and, as a result, the girls were more receptive. This has continued to be a feature of all the British women's training squads.

Signs of Change

The inaugural World Championships for Women in 1980 in New York went well for Britain. The squad returned with no less than five medals, including the gold medal in the under 48 kilos category from Jane Bridge, who also won the stylist award.

To my mind, the medals were tangible signs that the change in women's judo in Britain, at least at the top level, was taking place. Mistakes were being made, but valuable lessons were being learned and put into practice. Among these was the gradual awareness that some throws were, by their very nature, more suited to women than others. Being short on upper body strength, women automatically felt more comfortable with throws such as *Drop-knee Morote-seoi-nage*, *Tai-otoshi* and the range of ashiwaza such as *Kouchi-gari*, *Ouchi-gari* and *Kosoto-gari*, than with *Harai-goshi*, *Uchimata* and *Osoto-gari*.

I began to see that it was ludicrous to ask women to work hard on *Kata-guruma* or *Uranage* and expect reasonable results from the input. It was far more valuable to work on the lighter techniques and learn to perfect them on the move. The women may start their study of a throw standing still, but they must soon learn specific moving patterns in order to become adept at throwing when moving to the left or right, back or forwards, and in the half-circle.

By experimenting and closely monitoring the results, we discovered that certain techniques which logically should work, did not work in practice. For instance, *Tai-otoshi* and *Oguruma* worked well when performed on an opponent moving in a half-circle in the direction of tori's throwing side. But they didn't work so well for women when the opponent was moving in a half-circle but retreating. The reason for this is that at some point tori must stop the opponent with the force of the arms and bring her forward, which requires a man's order of strength rather than a woman's.

Practice with Juniors

It was during this same period that, by chance, we realised that major improvement was possible when the women stopped practising with men. Practising with other women was the ideal training, but in Britain, as elsewhere, women were still relatively few in numbers in the average judo club.

During 1982, in the preparation for the World Championships in Paris, I had most of my squad training with me in London on a daily basis, and the women began training with the older juniors. We discovered that 14, 15 or 16-year-old brown belts provided an ideal practice, for they were skilled, fast, fairly strong, but without a man's mature strength – and they were competitive in the best sense of the word. They knew they were competing with adult women who were among the best in the world, and it was no great blow to their ego to be bowled over by them, but it was an achievement if they managed to catch the women. So the randori was lively and inventive.

This was very different to the average practice with male Dan grades or brown belts. Although many men are aware of the kind of practice a woman needs and the kind of work they can do to make the practice worthwhile for them both, the majority of men are unaware of the implications of practising with a woman. They just do not want to be seen to be bowled over by a 'mere' woman or caught on the ground, so if danger threatens they 'close up' the practice by making their arms into iron bars. Thus, whereas my women's team could really learn with the schoolboys, against men randori was more a test of survival.

International Competition

With gold medals from Karen Briggs and Loretta Doyle, and a bronze medal from Diane Bell, the Paris World Championships were further proof that our training methods were on the right track. It was also becoming evident, however, that the rest of the world was catching up. Understandably, the competitive nature of international sport judo meant that each country was extremely protective of its hard-won information in the pioneering days of women's judo. Each coach and trainer, and the women themselves, were working out new ideas, now that they had accepted the basic concept that women's judo was different to men's and not just a form of lightweight judo. While we would meet and talk at the international events, none of the coaches of the main countries, such as Great Britain, France, Austria, West Germany and the USA, would reveal too much of their training methods or training ideas. This meant that everyone probably made many of the same mistakes, but it also meant that different solutions were found to the same problems.

Britain became known for producing girls who could throw extremely well with a variety of techniques, but whose newaza was not, generally, of the same standard. It was this area that needed attention after Paris.

Weight Training

Although certain things were working particularly well for women, there were still problems in practising them. While it was now easier for women to get worthwhile groundwork practice from men, there was still a reluctance on the men's part not to use brute strength when they were about to be held down – so the holds were the weakest part of the British squad's newaza skills.

At this time we began to experiment with weight training for women. We tried out various weights programmes in addition to the fitness programmes which were still in the developing stage, and carefully monitored the results. We noticed that there was a substantial and almost immediate benefit in groundwork practice among the women who had worked on the weights, although it needed to be balanced by extensive technical study.

Weights also had an effect on standing work. Initially the speed did drop, but the long-term effect of increased strength factors meant that, at last, some of the women could realistically begin to attempt important contest throws such as *Uchimata* – although the emphasis remained on throwing on the move. So another guideline was established, but movement again was the key.

CONCLUSIONS

All these guidelines were established over a period of years, but within the hothouse of the squad system. We endeavoured to introduce the ideas in coaching seminars and courses throughout the country, but even now it is clear that many of the basic concepts have not reached grass-roots level. It may take another decade for this to happen, and perhaps the face of women's judo will only really change when the top women, who have themselves learned this way, stop competing and become teachers. By that time, a whole new superstructure of ideas will probably have been built on the base that was established in the first decade of major international championships for women. The greater attention paid to women's judo by the Soviet Union and Japan following its inclusion in the Olympic programme will, alone, give a totally new impetus to the sport.

Yet it must not be forgotten that even now most women and young girls take up judo because they want to learn to defend themselves. That is also one reason why the drop-out rate is relatively high, although, perhaps surprisingly, it is not as high as in other combat systems. Few of the combat sports or martial arts are as realistic in training as judo, in which, relatively early on, women can see where they stand in relation to defending themselves against a large and aggressive man. Perhaps it is realism rather than pessimism that makes them turn to something else which is either more specific, like a self-defence course, or has a higher degree of fantasy, such as some of the more exotic combat systems that are now on sale. Many, however, do stay with judo because they are absorbed by the richness of technique and enjoy the ability to take the techniques to their limits, which is difficult to do with a system involving dangerous strikes or weapons. It says much for judo itself that so many do stay and survive all the inherent problems of practising with men and being taught by instructors who may be advanced in men's style, but who have little knowledge of the contemporary developments in women's judo.

There is a danger that with so much happening in the sport side of women's judo we forget that it comprises other equally important elements, such as self-defence and kata, and that it was designed by Jigoro Kano as an education to develop the personality. Sport competition is only one area of judo, though for a young judoka it may appear the most important.

Self-defence has an important role in women's judo. The experience of hard body contact that a female judoka receives is one of the most valuable lessons from which a woman can benefit in a truly practical approach to self-defence. Basic throws, basic groundwork throws, a basic ability not to freeze when grabbed by an aggressor – all these lessons are crucial in self-defence terms. A serious and realistic reassessment of the self-defence value of judo training for women is long overdue. When I think of the skills of some of the women who have trained on my mat, I can only conclude that a would-be rapist would get a terrific shock. Just as importantly, if those same women were caught and were assaulted I feel that they would have a much faster return to mental equilibrium than the majority of women.

All this points to the fact that the changing face of women's judo both on the domestic and international fronts is proving to be one of the most exciting developments in the combat sports as a whole. By the end of the twentieth century, I anticipate that not only will the practice of women have changed dramatically from the judo we now see in the average club, but that club membership will have substantially increased. The future of women's judo looks very positive indeed.

2 The History of Women's Judo

The growth of women's judo was bound to be fraught with difficulties, even though there were precedents in Japanese history of daughters as well as sons being instructed in the martial arts. The popularity of the naginata as a weapon for women remains even in twentieth-century Japan, as well as kyudo (the way of archery) and other weapon-based systems. There are also records of some women being brought up in the ju jitsu tradition. There was, however, a general reluctance among men to involve women in judo, stemming partly from the view that women could not hope to match the strength of men and therefore would necessarily be inferior. This was based on a fixed idea of the efficacy of judo *per se* – in other words, that in order for it to be a real practice, rather than a hobby or a pastime, it had to work in real circumstances. That meant it had to work at least against the average man in the dojo, and it was unlikely that most women could live up to this.

Another prejudice which hampered the development of women's judo was the view of many men that certain activities were more appropriate to women than others. It was appropriate, in Japanese society, for a woman to practise ikebana (flower arrangement) or chado (the tea ceremony), but not judo which would involve her in unsightly movements: the Japanese (and many Westerners later on) did not feel it was right for women to grovel on the ground. Why this was more acceptable for men was generally unexplained. Behind all this was the established Japanese social order where women, in many ways, were classed as secondary citizens, although it must be remembered that throughout Japanese history women have been among the leading poets and writers, so their status has not always been as subservient as their attitude and language might suggest.

THE INFLUENCE OF JIGORO KANO

Thus, in 1882, when Jigoro Kano created Kodokan judo from his studies in various ju jitsu schools, the attitude towards women was somewhat ambivalent. In the very early days, the number of men studying judo was small and, presumably, the question of whether women should or should not practise was not so much of an issue. This was underlined by the rigorous practice in the early days which also involved some very real feuds with other ju jitsu schools, ending on occasions not only in severe injuries, but also in death.

Although Kano is best known in the West as the founder of judo, he was himself a highly educated man and the principal of one of the leading Japanese universities; education of the individual was the central concept of his life, not a martial arts practice. He would undoubtedly have regretted being remembered only as the creator of a sport.

Kano regarded his judo not just as a physical or self-defence training but as an education in a much broader sense. It was designed to be a medium for the development of

Girls practising with Kano.

character and a clear attitude to life as much as a method of developing physical skills. The way women's judo developed in those first decades in Japan indicated that Kano himself was initially unsure of the role women should or could play in judo. He obviously saw that, in principle, women would benefit from judo in the broader character terms in much the same way as men – even if they could not compete with men on equal terms.

In his own book on judo Kano discusses its various aspects, including judo and physical education, randori, kata, judo and mental training, and aesthetic in judo. In this last section he remarks:

'There is that love of beauty and delight to be derived from assuming graceful attitudes and performing graceful movements, and in seeing and appreciating these qualities in others. The training in them, together with the pleasure obtainable from watching graceful movements symbolical of different ideas, constitutes what we call the emotional or aesthetic side of judo.'

Some eleven years after the founding of Kodokan Judo, Kano first began to instruct a group of women led by one Kayatani Sueko, although this seems to have been an unofficial class. There is also an account of a series of private lessons Kano himself gave to a Miss Yasuda in 1904. For the first month Miss Yasuda did not wear a judogi and practised only *Ju-no-kata* and some physical exercises. During the second month she practised only breakfalls. This was followed by a physical examination in hospital to ensure that she had not overtaxed herself, and only then was she allowed to do technical work and throw for throw practice.

It was not until 1923, years after Kano's unofficial lessons, that the instruction of women in judo was started formally. This indicates the enormous reluctance on the part of the judo hierarchy to admit women into judo at all; and when a women's section was opened it was separate from the men's and more limited in its training structure.

In 1926 a conference on women's judo was followed by the foundation of the Women's section of the Kodokan and the establishment of the principles of women's judo, which were to hold sway, largely unchanged, for nearly half a century. Women could learn judo

Kata practice.

Girls practising randori.

through technique training, light randori, kata and self-defence exercises, but there was to be no arduous randori and certainly no competition. Through this training the early Japanese pioneers of women's judo must have been technically accomplished – at least in an academic sense. Constant practice of *Ju-no-kata* and *Kime-no-kata* must have given the women much of the flavour of judo, although whether it really satisfied those instincts which made them take up the activity in the first place will never be known. The nature of the society in which they grew up meant that women were unlikely to question the limits which had been forced upon them.

It was not until 1933 that the first woman, Kozaki Kaneko, was promoted to 1st Dan. Her black belt, however, had a white stripe through the middle – a ruling introduced by men in order to distinguish a woman's grade from a man's grade. This was adopted by Americans but was never widespread in Europe, although it was occasionally seen and in the 1960s made a temporary appearance in Britain.

JUDO IN EUROPE

By this time the initiative for the development of women's judo had passed abroad, particularly to England where, in Europe at least, judo had taken root most strongly through the efforts of two Japanese emigrants, Gunji Koizumi, founder of Europe's first judo club, The Budokwai, and his chief instructor Yukio Tani.

In fact, judo has been practised by women in England since shortly after touring Japanese ju jitsu/judo exponents first demonstrated their skills in Europe. In a truly extraordinary book written in 1906 by Mrs Emily Watts and dedicated 'with grateful affection' to Her Grace, the Duchess of Bedford, *The Fine Art of Jujutsu* is expounded in an admirably clear manner – by women. Showing unusual deference for a Japanese man, one of the first teachers in Europe, Mr Raku Uyenishi, is shown as uke in certain throws 'too severe for ordinary pupils to take on the lawn' being thrown by Mrs Watts herself. For the most

The first position of Ashiharai *showing the foot being tripped from behind.*

The first position of Hikiotoshi *showing the different position of the thrower's left foot.*

part, however, the book seems to have been put together by women for a general audience; and although some of the clothes would look rather strange in the modern dojo, most of the techniques would not. It is interesting to note that although the book dates from 1906, Mrs Watts describes in some detail a *Nage-no-kata* 'from the Kano School' where *Sukui-nage* is used in place of the *Kata-guruma* used now.

Although Mrs Watts talks in terms of '*Landori-Kata*', it seems that most of her training was done in kata form rather than free-fighting randori. However, she does suggest that the throws are practised in 'loose play' which indicates that, despite the hair in buns and the legs in bloomers, judo was a more action-packed activity for women in the first few years of the twentieth century in England than it was for Japanese women for decades afterwards. Incidentally, Mrs Watts recommends after a bout of 'loose play' a long cool drink, then a warm bath followed by a cold shower.

The Fine Art of Jujutsu indicates that judo interested European women in the early days, though it seemed to be a somewhat aristocratic or at least upper class pastime. This was also true of the first women members of The Budokwai. Miss Katharine White Cooper became the first woman to join The Budokwai when she signed her membership on 4 April 1919. The Budokwai records show Mrs H. Taylor also paying her one guinea membership in December, and in the 1920s others joined, though by this time the cost had risen to three guineas.

Women, however, remained a very small percentage of the total judo fraternity, even as judo became slightly more widely known in the West, helped by visits paid by Japanese teachers – one of the main results of Jigoro Kano's own visit to the Budokwai in 1920.

Although a few Englishmen had already trained at the Kodokan by this time, it wasn't until the mid 1930s that a woman, Mrs Yvonne Myers, a playwright, made the trip to Japan. It was about this time, too, that one of the most famous of all judo women in these early days, Dame Enid Russell-Smith, began judo at the age of 34. She was eventually to become the first woman outside Japan to reach the grade of 3rd Dan. Pursuing a successful career first as a civil servant and then as the principal of a college, Dame Enid Russell-Smith became particularly noted as the editor for some years of the *Budokwai Bulletin*. She was also filmed performing kata with Koizumi and other high grades in the immediate post-war era.

The Second World War had its effect on judo. In Japan the Kodokan was largely kept going by the women's section, but in the West judo came more or less to a standstill. Though there had been various competitions between England, Germany, France and others in the 1920s and 1930s, only men had been involved: there were simply no competitions for women.

The post-war period saw a great expansion of judo in many European countries. In

The second position of the Koshiharai *showing the force with which the opponent's legs are thrown up into the air.*

France, West Germany and Britain women began to be seen more frequently as judo started to reach a wider cross-section. There was no real awareness of a different approach being necessary and in Britain, at least, a certain amount of male reluctance in the dojo was imported from Japan – though some would argue that it was inherent in the British attitude anyway.

In The Budokwai, in London, a Ladies' Class was formed in the late 1940s taken by Dame Enid Russell-Smith. This continued well into the 1960s, when the club moved to its current premises and the class was taken by the most successful English woman judoka of the time, Christine Child. Memories of the class by prominent figures indicate that the segregation was worthwhile in the long run for it did mean that women could practise with each other on their own terms, rather than having to endure an unequal battle with men, some of whom were reluctant to practise with women and lacked understanding.

The difficulties stemmed from the fact that the Ladies' Class was confined to a small dojo, which was inadequate even for the relatively small numbers that used to practise regularly. Generally, women were not encouraged to practise upstairs in the main dojo, unless, like Christine Child (who went on to win the over 72 kilos title in the first European Championships in 1975), they had attained a high standard.

In fact, many of the top British male grades simply refused to teach women, both in and out of London. This was true well into the 1950s and even early 1960s, even though by this time it was quite common to see women on the mat with men. The numbers of women practising, however, were still relatively small; for example, in Britain in 1961 there were just twelve women Dan grades. Some of these top women were becoming aware of different possibilities in approaching techniques; Ivy Armitage used to comment that the emphasis in *Harai-goshi* when performed by a man was clearly placed on the shoulders, but

An armlock defence against a push. Note the defender's left arm locked tightly on to the attacker's right, just above his elbow.

when performed by a woman the emphasis lay in the work done by the hips.

Women largely had to learn to survive. One account recalls a rather brusque introduction to judo where the class started with 45 minutes of hard exercises, concluding in heaving an 11lb medicine ball around the mat 'to build up strength'. To survive that particular ladies' class (held as part of a judo club in an industrial firm) individuals had to be strongly attracted to judo – not surprisingly, the drop-out rate was very high.

JUDO IN THE USA

The situation in the United States was even more difficult. Rusty Kanokogi, whose remarkably strong personality resulted in the promotion of the first World Championships for Women in New York in 1980, recalls the immense difficulties she had in even getting started. When in 1955 she finally managed to persuade the instructor of the local dojo to let her train, she discovered she was the only woman among forty men. The handful of other women she met in New York practising judo appeared to follow the Japanese women's tradition and limited themselves to kata. This was not the Kanokogi style. She took part in interclub competitions, fighting against men and doing well, and was predictably incensed that no competitions for women existed. So she taped her breasts flat, cut her hair short, entered the New York State YMCA Championships as a man and won her weight category. When the news eventually leaked out, her victories were cancelled and her medal was taken away. As a result, officials quickly inserted 'male' into the event title so that she could not enter again.

That was 1958, and it was a decade before women's contests appeared as a regular feature of the American judo scene. By that time, Rusty Kanokogi had claimed other 'firsts'. In 1962 she went to Japan to study further at the Kodokan and was horrified at the limited practice she discovered in the women's section. After one week with the women, she became the first woman to be invited to practise with the men in the main dojo.

Rusty Kanakogi.

COMPETITION IN EUROPE

The competitive scene in Britain was slightly more developed than that in the USA. By the late 1950s the increased prominence of women in judo could no longer be ignored. The British Judo Association was being pressed for proper provision for women, and the First Association Coaching Conference for Women took place in 1959. This was followed, in 1961, by the formation of a Ladies' Committee, with representatives from England, Scotland, Wales and Northern Ireland, the objective of which was to improve judo for women. It produced the first Association Syllabus for Women and was replaced in 1964 by the National Women's Council of Great Britain. It was just a matter of time before competition for women was formally established.

The early 1960s saw some unofficial competitions take place. Women had contested in grade examinations for some time, but areas such as the northern Home Counties started to introduce women's events as part of the annual championships. Some of the higher graded women were also refereeing. The real breakthrough, however, came in 1966 with the first Team Championships for Women, linked to a kata competition, held at Liverpool University. Just how reluctant the male hierarchy in judo was to accede to the demand for women's competitions can be seen by the conditions to which the women were forced to adhere.

For a start, the competition had to take place behind closed doors and only invited observers were allowed to watch. Even more ludicrous was the edict that although ippons and waza-aris would form the basis of wins and losses, marks were also awarded by the judges in each fight for skill, style, the quality of general movement and spirit. These extra marks could, and did, affect the results of individual contests.

The success of the competition, however, was beyond doubt, and it was repeated in 1968, this time at Keele University, with the same patronising rule concerning extra marks for skill and style. The only slight change was that tickets for the competition could be bought in advance by the general public, although, for some reason, tickets could not be bought on the day. In 1969 the event was transferred to Crystal Palace because of its success, but male sensitivities still existed and the contest area was shielded from casual view by a special, heavy curtain.

The impetus created by these events led inevitably to the first British Open Championships for Women, held at Bracknell in 1971. This was arguably the first international competition for women to be held anywhere in the world. West Germany sent a women's team, Holland sent observers, and there was a total of 110 entries.

The following year saw a major expansion. No fewer than nine countries took part, with representatives from Austria, West Germany, Switzerland, Sweden, Holland, England, Scotland, Northern Ireland and Wales. International women's judo was now definitely established. In 1973 the event moved to Crystal Palace, and women from the USA, Italy and France were among the additional visitors.

At the same time national squads in the leading European judo countries were being formed (Britain's squad was established in 1972) and pressure mounted for the creation of an annual European Championships. A trial event was held in Genoa, Italy, in 1974, and the first official European Championships for Women took place in Munich in 1975. Women's judo had arrived.

These international events seemed to open the floodgates for women's judo. The first major competition for women in France did not take place until as late as 1973 (in Lausanne), with further experimental events leading up to the first official French Championships for Women in 1974. The first National Championships for Women in the United States also took place in 1974, in Phoenix, and three years later it was followed by the first Pan American Women's Championships.

The growth of women's judo throughout the Western world can be seen by the increase in the numbers of women Dan grades in Britain. In 1958 there were just ten women Dan grades, and any women's grading over orange belt had to be carefully organised beforehand with women being brought in from quite a wide area. By 1976 the number of women Dan grades in British clubs had risen to 303, with five 4th Dans. By 1986 the figure had topped the 700 mark.

INTERNATIONAL RECOGNITION

The growing importance of women's judo internationally could not be ignored by the International Judo Federation. As early as 1972 there had been a proposal from Italy to the IJF Congress that a women's championships should be held. Even in Japan changes of attitude were clearly taking place. In 1968 an 'investigation' had begun into women's competition, and in 1972 the first test competitions were carried out in the Kodokan's women's section, although it was not until 1978 that the first National Women's Championships were held in Japan. It was this same year that marked the general introduction of competition-style randori for women in Japan.

As the first unofficial European Championships were being held in Genoa in 1974, so the first Oceanic Women's Judo Championships were taking place. There were also Open Championships for Women in West Germany and Switzerland, while Italy, Czechoslovakia and Holland were establishing equally popular events for women. It was the success of the Genoa European Championships that prompted the IJF to issue the historic ruling in November 1974 to the effect that: 'If Women's Judo Championships are conducted successfully by at least three Continental Unions, the IJF will duly consider sponsoring World Women's Judo Championships, and also including Women's Judo Championships in the Olympic Games.'

It took six years and the unquenchable energy of one woman finally to make this happen. Rusty Kanokogi made judo history throughout her life, both in America and Japan, as she battled her way past the doors of prejudice: the staging of the World Judo Championships was her greatest success. They took place in New York in December 1980, after nine months of ceaseless work in finding sponsors and attracting the attention of women judoka throughout the world. The Championships were a triumph, with 149 athletes from 27 countries and a thousand spectators on each of the two days. This further emphasised the significance of women in judo in world terms, and there has been a World Championships for Women at a regular two-year interval since.

Still there was prejudice. Despite the undeniable success of the first World Championships, Rusty Kanokogi found herself forced into action less than twelve months later, when the US Olympic Committee and the largely male-dominated US Judo Inc. excluded women from the 1981 National Sports Festival. Mrs Kanokogi filed a sex-discrimination complaint against the two organisations, which, together with the publicity that ensued, finally allowed the doors of prejudice, in the United States at least, to be partially opened, and the proper funding of women's judo finally began.

The manner in which Britain had led the world in terms of women's competition suggested that the really entrenched attitudes had been swept aside as the first World Championships approached. This was not so. The Women's Team managers, first Elizabeth Viney, followed by Maria Fourt and then Roy Inman, were expected to work for nothing (as Rusty Kanokogi was in the United States) for no one in the male-dominated British Judo Association had made formal application to the appropriate grant-funding bodies.

In 1979 women's judo hit the headlines when the British Judo Association was taken to court for discrimination by not allowing a fully qualified national referee to referee men's national competitions – just because that referee was a woman. The individual concerned, Belinda Petty, won her case in the Industrial Tribunal. The BJA opposed her with the ludicrous argument that were two heavyweights to lose their temper in a contest a woman would be unable to separate them and restore order. Considering the size and temperament of many male referees, it is

Karen Briggs.

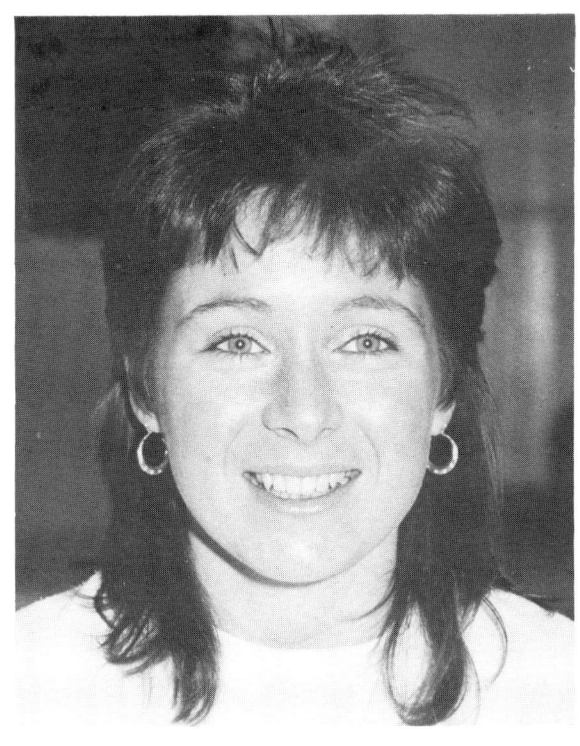

Loretta Doyle.

Brigitte Deydier.

Ingrid Berghmans.

difficult to see what they would do in such a case either. When the BJA lost its case, it took the matter to Appeal and lost again. Only then did it let the matter drop.

It is worth noting, however, that even in the middle 1980s there are only three women referees with full national qualifications in the UK, and only one with an IJF qualification. Women referees are rarely seen on the mat of a women's World Championship, although men dominate in women's World Championship events.

THE END OF SEGREGATION

The growth in importance of women's judo internationally coincided with the increasing significance of the time factor in the international sports arena. In the major sports of athletics and swimming, men's and women's competitions were not segregated. The change from a woman's event to a man's event varied the pace and the interest, and increased its attractiveness as a spectator sport.

The strength of judo relies very much on its broad base as a participatory activity, but there was no real reason why women's judo should not take place in the same arena as men's. This already happened on a local level in clubs and areas, but the national and international events were strictly segregated. This barrier was gradually broken down, with the major breakthrough again taking place in Britain.

Judo appeared in the programme of the Commonwealth Games for the first time in Edinburgh in 1986. It was classed as a demonstration event, but was scheduled for the main programme in 1990. Despite its secondary status as a demonstration event, it proved one of the most successful of the Games – partly due to the fact that, for the first time in a major international, the individual men's event and the individual women's event were held concurrently, with two mats for each.

Neither women's judo nor men's judo suffered from the comparison, which highlighted the differences rather than any superiority or inferiority in technique. The manner in which the spectator's interest was sustained by a top competitor in the women's event followed by a top competitor in the men's made the day one of the most exciting judo events of the year.

This pattern is clearly to be the form of the future, as the international competition schedule has brought together the men's and women's European events from 1987, and similarly the World Championships in the same year.

OLYMPIC ACCEPTANCE

This international ending of segregation was partly prompted by the imminent inclusion of women's judo in the main sporting event of the globe, the Olympic Games. This was the one major bastion that women's judo had yet to penetrate. Here, it was not just a question of male indifference. With the danger of the whole event growing to elephantine proportions, with scores of sports clamouring for acceptance, the Olympic Committee was desperately trying to trim down the programme, not expand it. Hopes had been raised that women's judo would be on the programme in 1980, but they were not realised, and there was disappointment again when the Los Angeles Games in 1984 came and went without women's representation.

Once again the doughty Rusty Kanokogi maintained her pressure, but this time she was backed by the IJF. A 25,000 signature petition for women's inclusion was sent to the International Olympic Committee President Juan Samaranch, and once again threatened litigation, this time against ABC-TV for entering into a contract with an organisation (the IOC) that allegedly discriminates against women. Finally even the IOC relented, although only in part. Women's judo was to be accepted on to the Olympic programme in 1988 as a demonstration event, with full inclusion in 1992.

Although this two-part entry seems somewhat nonsensical, it means that women's judo as a sport will gain the ultimate official recognition for which it has fought for so long. It has taken over 100 years, since the foundation of judo itself, for women's judo to come of age, and the closing years of this century will prove extremely interesting. For Olympic acceptance has meant that at last the major sporting countries of the Eastern bloc – particularly the Soviet Union and East Germany – have begun to devote time, interest and money to women's judo. In the same way that men's judo technically took a leap forward when the Soviet Union entered international judo in the 1960s, much the same can be expected in women's judo, although it will take two Olympiads or so.

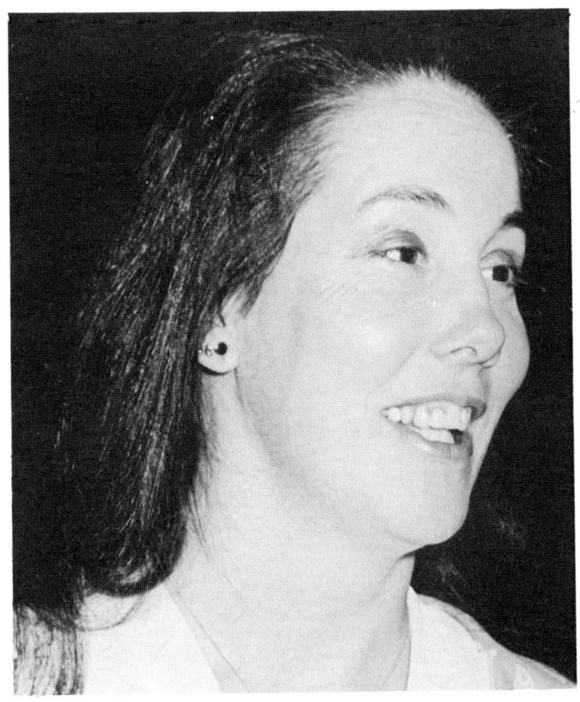

Christine Childs.

EUROPEAN DOMINATION

It has been significant that to date the women's European Championships and the World Championships have been dominated by remarkably few countries. Austria, West Germany, France, Britain and Italy have taken the bulk of the medals, but by the start of the 1980s other countries, such as Poland, were making a noticeable impact.

The events have produced outstanding individuals. Ingrid Berghmans, the Belgian light heavyweight, showed extraordinary skill, consistency and determination in winning the open category in the first three World Championships, as well as her own weight category in the 1984 event in Vienna; and added to that three European titles.

Austrian Edith Hrovat won the under 48 kilos category in the European Championships in 1975 and was still competing successfully in 1986, having accumulated no less than eight European titles; while her compatriot Gerda Winklbauer notched up one world title and five European titles.

Britain, too, has produced a string of outstanding competitors. Jane Bridge not only won the U48k category in the first World Championships in New York in 1980, but was also given the stylist of the event award. She was followed by the remarkable talent of Karen Briggs, who won the same category on the following three consecutive occasions, as well as five European titles over the period. In fact, the 1986 World Championships in Maastricht, Holland, saw no fewer than three world titles going to Britain, with Karen Briggs retaining her U48k title, and Ann Hughes and Diane Bell winning the U56k and U61k categories respectively.

France showed its strength in the women's section with outstanding competitors such as three-times world champion Brigitte Deydier (U66k) and Beatrice Rodriguez, who also has world and European titles to her credit.

This dominance of the medals in major

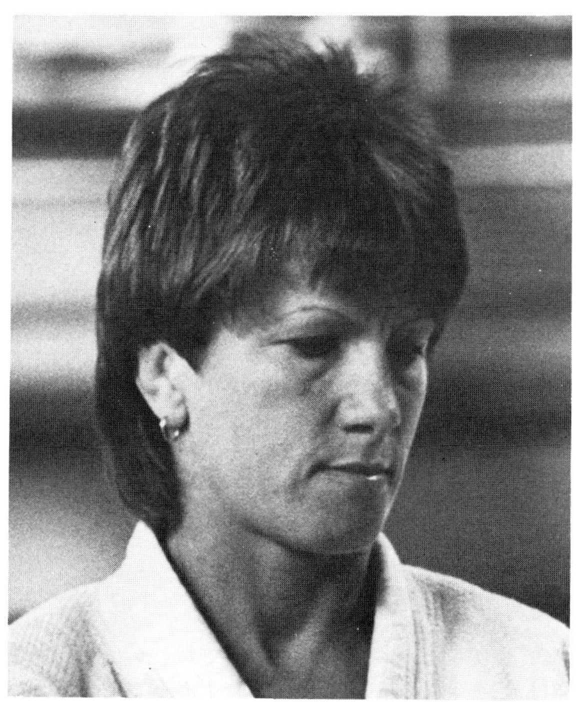

Edith Hrovat.

Jane Bridge.

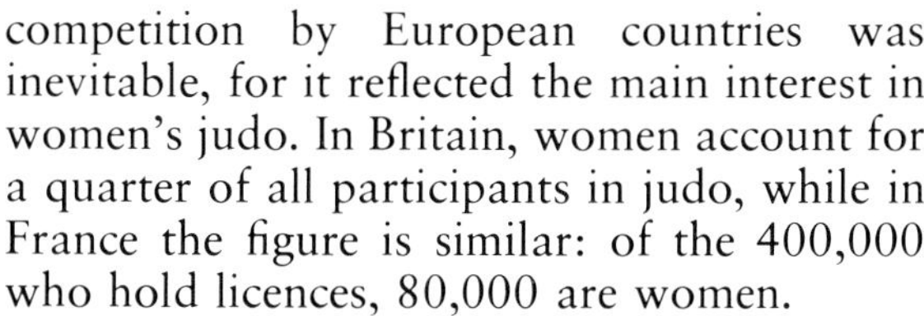

competition by European countries was inevitable, for it reflected the main interest in women's judo. In Britain, women account for a quarter of all participants in judo, while in France the figure is similar: of the 400,000 who hold licences, 80,000 are women.

In the first World Championships, only one Japanese, Kaori Yamaguchi, figured in the medal tables, and she had to wait until 1984 before she won a gold medal. This again reflects the state of women's competitive judo in the sport's home country. This is, however, rapidly changing; at the time of writing there are seven universities with women's sections in the judo faculties, although this is still remarkably small. The annual Fukuoka Tournament for Women is also proving to be one of the finest in the international programme, even though, once again, European women dominate.

Women's judo is still developing rapidly. Standards are rising, the range of techniques is increasing, and the number of events is growing. Junior events, too, are becoming more established as countries aiming for sporting excellence and sporting success see the need to gain international experience at a good level at an earlier age.

Just how far women's judo has come in the lifetime of one judoka has been truly extraordinary. Those few women who in the post-war period bravely stepped on to men's judo mats in West Germany, France, the USA, Great Britain, Holland, Italy and other countries would not have believed that such drastic changes could occur in so short a time. There is no doubt that the days when women could be regarded as a novelty or a nuisance and definitely inferior in judo technique and knowledge are over. Women's judo is here to stay.

3 Tachiwaza

SEOI-NAGE
ASHIWAZA
TOMOE-NAGE
HIP TECHNIQUES
TAI-OTOSHI
OTHER DIRECT ATTACKS
COMBINATIONS
COUNTERS

Introduction

It could be argued that the vast riches contained in the throwing skills of judo are unmatched by any sport. The array of different classes of throws – hand throws, foot throws, hip throws, sacrifice throws, counters and combinations – and the different directions in which they can be made make tachiwaza an absorbing and a lifetime's study. There are throws more appropriate for reckless youth; throws for the mature stateswomen of judo; throws for the light and fast, the tall and strong, the compact and the lanky. In a judo career, it is possible to go through a range of throws as personal circumstances such as age, fitness and ambitions change. Apart from occasional dull times, which are often reflections of problems in other areas of life – in that sense judo is a good barometer of one's personal state at any one moment in time – it should not be possible to become bored with judo.

However, it is just this immense variety that can be confusing at the beginning of a judo career, and indeed at all the stages along the way. With such a plethora of possibilities among the throwing techniques, where does one begin? How real this problem is can be seen in the fact that despite a century of intensive practice throughout the world there is no universally accepted beginning; nor is there an agreed order of throws, in terms of difficulty or merit, or even in terms of the skills learned. The only basic guideline that can be given is that throws from one leg are more difficult than throws on two legs, although there are sufficient exceptions to raise doubts over even this simple statement.

Nevertheless, it seems clear that after ten years or so of organised major international competitions for women, there appears to be a preference for the stable throws, those which are made from two legs or two feet – *Ogoshi*, *Tai-otoshi* or *Drop Seoi-nage* – rather than *Uchimata* or *Osoto-gari*. Natural affinity can make nonsense of this rule and there are other classes of throw, such as sacrifice throws (which could be regarded as the most stable of all), which confuse the issue. It is, however, one of the basic factors to take into consideration when deciding what kind of personal pattern should be created from the rich palette of tachiwaza that is on offer.

There is no question that after a short period of training – perhaps a year or two – it is necessary to think in terms of developing a pattern of technique that suits one's individual circumstances. Size, age, goals, frequency of practice, fitness – all these aspects must be taken into account when considering systematising the training pattern.

Establishing a Tachiwaza Pattern

Most judoka need at least three major techniques in their repertoire, techniques that they have studied in depth and both understand and enjoy, and with which they can achieve ippon. These techniques may change in order of preference or effectiveness, and occasionally, in top competition, they may cease to work for a short while for no apparent reason. They are there as the foundation of the individual's tachiwaza, and from those three techniques all other standing work evolves. As a judo career progresses, those main techniques will change to match the new circumstances; but it is important that everyone – at least all Dan grades – is clear which are the three main techniques in the repertoire at any one time.

Choosing those techniques is not a simple task, nor can it be done in one session at a desk with a paper and pencil. They emerge from personal preference, from admiring the technique when done by others, from a natural affinity demonstrated in randori; or they can be suggested by an instructor or coach, or even selected intellectually as the answer to a particularly difficult opponent or kinds of opponents.

The three techniques need not be interconnected, although invariably, during the course of the study, a good Dan grade will discover ways of connecting those techniques which have not, perhaps, been seen before. Nevertheless, they should encompass attacks to both left and right sides, and should contain opportunities for dealing with the variety of sizes of opponents who are likely to be encountered. It is not advisable to attempt techniques which are not suited to your body stature. For example, if you are short and squat *Osoto-gari* will probably be of little use. However, if you can develop the throw, it will really surprise your opponents.

The development of these main techniques does not happen overnight. The process of adding a new major throw to a judoka's repertoire is a long one and can take a year or more. The first stage is to work on static uchikomi, just getting the feel of the basic movement. Then there comes a kata-style uchikomi, with perhaps one or two steps introducing the element of movement and establishing a study of timing. Gradually a familiarity with the movement will mean that the technique can be introduced into randori, first of all against less experienced partners, then, little by little, against more equal opposition. It can take six months to reach the stage when the throw begins to work fairly regularly in randori, for this is the time necessary to develop muscle memory, where, once initiated, the movement will begin to take care of itself.

There will naturally be many frustrating times, particularly when regular training partners become aware of the emerging throw. They can learn more quickly how to stifle it than you can learn how to make it effective. It is here that one or two small 'bristling' combinations, judiciously introduced, can divert their attention from the main purpose of the practice.

After about a year the technique will begin to work in competition. Sometimes this stage comes more quickly, sometimes more slowly, and sometimes it never comes which is hard luck. At some point the technique may need to be discarded. However, a serious study will always prove beneficial in the long run – spin-off benefits can come from the most unexpected quarters.

Attached to each of the chosen techniques should be a range of smaller attacks that can be used in combination: as an entry into the big throw or as an exit from a failed attempt at the big throw. In fact, those three techniques should be bristling with combination possibilities, although there should be a clear distinction between the small sting and the ippon-scorer. That doesn't mean that it is impossible to score ippon with the smaller attacks. In randori and contest opponents will often defend so strongly against the known big throw that they leave themselves wide open for the smaller attack.

Specific programmes for fitness, tactics, stances, combinations and defences should be built around these three main techniques. For example, if *Te-guruma* is one of the chosen three the individual could undertake a weight-training programme; she must develop ways of inducing her opponent to attack to create the opportunity for *Te-guruma* as a counter; she must learn to 'ride' throws well so that she has confidence in letting opponents attack in order to effect her counter.

This kind of intricate preparation is necessary for a top competitor, who has the advantage of being able to train full time. But it also applies, though perhaps with less detail, to the club player, the recreational judoka. She, too, will gain more satisfaction from her judo by creating order and purpose in her training. She will be able to devise ways of supporting her chosen techniques by making imaginative use both of her training time and everyday life – whether it is by lifting ordinary items in a way which matches her required judo movement or by using stairs as part of her fitness training. The key is to live an ordinary life with a judo awareness.

In the long term, a concentration on just three main techniques teaches an individual the content of judo. It teaches awareness of balance, balance of the individual and balance of the opponent. It teaches principles of throwing, principles of controlling an opponent, of directing a throw, of using a small throw to enter for a large throw. Once three throws have been thoroughly studied, the acquisition of other throwing skills becomes relatively easy because the individual is, by then, a practising judoka.

Important Points

Concentration on three throws does not mean that the wide range of other tachiwaza should be neglected. It could be argued that a good standard competitor should be conversant with 100 judo techniques and be able to demonstrate them to an adequate standard with a willing uke. These 100 techniques should include basic throws, combinations and counters, and should cover the range of classes of throw. From this will come a fluency of action in randori and competition.

Despite all the training and preparation it is possible that an opponent of equal ability will prevent all attempts to throw, and it is at this point that a broader understanding of judo can produce something special. It may come from a rapid analysis of the situation, but more often than not it just happens – a throw which one rarely practises spontaneously appears: it is the right throw for that opponent at that time, and the body, taught by the hours of experience, knows it. This is judo.

Tip

Developing tachiwaza obviously involves throwing. The traditional Japanese idea of 100,000 repetitions being needed before a throw begins to come naturally may have a touch of the Biblical forty days and forty nights about it, but there is certainly no doubt that in the end you need a willing partner. That partner will, no doubt, want an uke in return. So ukemi (breakfalls) are of fundamental significance.

There is no reason why good use should not be made of a crash mat. In the end, however, there is no substitute for a freely-moving practice, where training partners can roam the dojo, throwing at will, without worrying about having to aim for a certain spot. This is why good ukemi are vital to the development of throwing skills. It is nonsense to say that practising ukemi teaches the individual how to lose. Learning how to turn out of throws is another skill altogether and should be studied specifically.

Confident, fluent ukemi are a safety factor that should not be neglected, and their very simplicity helps towards the development of spatial awareness in the air.

SEOI-NAGE

Morote-seoi-nage   Double Lapel Drop Seoi-nage
Eri-seoi-nage   Morote-seoi-nage-makikomi
Drop Ippon-seoi-nage   Ippon-seoi-nage Arm Trap
Biceps Seoi-otoshi

Introduction

In its two major forms of *Morote-seoi-nage* and *Ippon-seoi-nage*, the shoulder throw as it is popularly called (though a literal translation is closer to back-carry) is without question the most important class of throw in women's judo. This is the throw that is attempted more than any other and is one of the most successful.

Just why this should be so is not entirely clear. It may be simply because it is one of the first throws taught to women. It can easily be proved how judoka, under the pressure of contest, revert to the first technique they learned, or at least the first technique with which they had success.

On the other hand, it may be the product of hours spent doing randori and even uchikomi with much taller and stronger men in the formative judo years. Both *Morote-seoi-nage* and *Ippon-seoi-nage* are obvious techniques to resort to if a 56 kilo woman finds herself face to face with a 78 kilo man, even if the man is a good uke. It is a far more practical technique to work on in those circumstances than, say, *Osoto-gari* or *Uchimata*. The woman can feel she is developing aspects of the throw and can complete the technique with a reasonable uke, whereas with a big *Uchimata* the man may be hesitant to go over well because he is not quite sure whether the woman will be able to support his weight. The last thing he wants is to find her collapsing underneath him, because the timing or balance was incorrect.

So, the *Seoi-nage* becomes a safe throw to attempt not just from the point of view of injury, but also, in randori, because it is a relatively difficult throw to counter.

The *Seoi-nage* is always taught as a standing throw, yet it is usually executed in contest as a dropping throw. Even in randori it is rare to see a truly committed *Seoi-nage* which is not 'dropped'. This applies as much to men as to women: *Drop Seoi-nage* is a crucially important throw in men's judo from about 86 kilos and below. Although they appear to be the same throw, the emphasis is very different. Men naturally call upon their upper body power to pull the opponent over while driving up from underneath; in the hands of a skilled man the *Drop Seoi-nage* can be a very powerful throw indeed.

Women, however, have evolved their own version, one that involves more rolling or rotational action, for they cannot rely on strong shoulders and biceps to turn the defensive opponent over the top; nor have they much ability to explode from underneath to give some height to the throw, although this can be improved by specific training.

The principal strength of the *Drop Seoi-nage* is its surprise factor. You are walking around with your opponent safely secured on the end of your strong arms, when suddenly the whole weight of your opponent drops at your feet and pulls you over. This tends to happen in men's judo from an eyeball to eyeball, static situation, but the best results for women come from a moving situation. One moment you are moving around feeling in control, and the next moment you find yourself being tipped into space.

This throw, above all, enables women to evade the defence of the strong arm, which is another reason for its popularity. It is the sudden twist and drop of body weight that effectively break uke's control and simultaneously pull uke off balance – or at least it has this potential. In a sense, the skilfully executed drop can be regarded as a bypass operation, negating defence.

The skill factor is very important. Few throws have been more misused than *Drop Seoi-nage* and few have been more maligned. The whole flop and drop syndrome, which gave such a bad name to women's judo (and junior judo for that matter) for so many years, emerged from an ill-considered and ill-timed use of this throw.

The general pattern is this: *Seoi-nage* is taught in either its *Morote* or *Ippon* form as a standing technique and is actually very rarely taught as a dropping technique. Both children and adults, however, soon learn that against an opponent of equal stature a standing *Seoi-nage* is extremely difficult. They see others achieving some success with dropping attempts, begin to imitate them and have some success themselves, for the surprise factor does produce good results. But often they never really study the mechanics of the *Drop Seoi-nage*, and as the surprise factor lessens, both in randori and in contest, so the failure rate rises.

In women's judo the best results from dropping *Seoi-nage* are achieved in a moving situation. The failure rate increases when tori turns in for a *Drop Seoi-nage* against a static opponent. In this situation the opponent can see it coming and, keeping the attacker at arm's length, just goes down with her to the ground. No score is given yet it looks like a bona fide attack, and even if the results are not manifested on the scoreboard the referee and corner judges notch up a mark for the *Drop Seoi* attempt. At this point the technique becomes a tactical ploy to notch up advantages. Tori looks active and uke looks passive, when in fact her intentions to set up her opponent for a real throw are being frustrated by continuous dropping attacks. This is 'flop and drop' *par excellence* and many a medal has been won by it – at all levels.

Basic Technique

Misuse of *Drop Seoi-nage* can be prevented by considering the technical implications of dropping. The sudden change of level from chest height (where the gripping dominates attention) to floor level (when the opponent twists and drops) should come as a total shock. This can be achieved, even when the opponent knows that a *Drop Seoi-nage* is coming, by combining perfect timing with a skilled movement on tori's part.

Tori must attempt the throw in a flurry of movement, preferably when uke is coming forward on to her right foot (for a right-handed technique). The twist and drop plants uke on her right foot, with tori, ideally, kneeling virtually between her feet. With uke slightly bending over from the gravitational pull, she has little chance of avoiding the technique.

There are, however, a number of factors crucial to the success of the throw in addition to timing. Tori must ensure that the control of uke's upper body has been maintained throughout the twist and drop. If a loose gap is allowed to appear, the dropping action can be stifled.

It is tori's arm control that creates the initial movement that brings uke round into position for an attack, and uke's arms that keep her there during the attack. But tori must be quite clear about how to drop.

The stepping action which brings most consistent success is the same for both *Morote* and *Ippon* forms of the *Drop Seoi-nage*. In a right-handed attack, tori must swing her left leg in a half-circle movement at great speed to bring her body round with her back to the opponent. But before that left leg hits the ground, tori must already be dropping. If she drops too early, she will not come far enough round. If she drops too late, she is telegraphing her intention to uke who can then simply step off the technique, because it is the drop that nails uke to the floor – before the rotation and throw.

Training

This dropping skill must be practised assiduously to avoid becoming just a flop and drop merchant, but the very nature of the technique makes standard uchikomi both difficult and wearing on the knees.

We have devised two methods to work on these aspects of dropping. The first is used when a small tori is partnered by a large uke, perhaps even by a man. Uke holds tori's belt and supports tori as she turns in, time and time again. Eventually they can develop a rhythm which allows uke to pull tori back on to her feet again, lessening the arduousness of the movement and the battering on the knees. In this repetition tori can concentrate on both her arm movements and her foot movements, as well as her general balance – she should not allow herself, for instance, to be pulled backwards. This is also a helpful exercise for uke, because she is becoming increasingly aware of the rapid change in the level of attack.

The second method is for tori to twist in and drop, but into a squat rather than on to her knees. This is excellent training in strengthening the thighs, but is rather tiring. It should be made clear that tori will not be expected to be able to throw from the full squat – few men can do that – although it can occasionally happen if the timing is perfect. The twist into a drop enables tori to develop her own spatial awareness of where she is in relation to the opponent she is throwing.

Direction

Until this point, we have been concerned with the entry to the throw rather than the throw itself, but the direction of the throw is as important to the ultimate success as the entry. You can do all the hard work of entering and setting up a good position, only to find it wasted by trying to throw in the wrong direction.

There are only two directions for a *Drop Seoi-nage*: straight over the top or (in a right-handed throw) to the right. It is important to train in both, using a crash mat and a willing partner, so that your body instinctively knows which is the right direction to throw – you will have no time to kneel and consider the options in the heat of contest.

The rule of thumb is that in your first attempt you aim for the full, straight-over-the-top movement. If your timing, positioning and body control are correct, uke will not be able to escape. However, if uke has managed to create a gap and come round to tori's right-hand side, tori must switch the attack to the right. What often happens in contest is that tori makes one attack, realises that this opponent is fast in evading the technique, and can aim for the right-hand direction of the throw in the next attempt. In effect it becomes a combination, for uke can be lulled into a false sense of security.

It may help to think of the two directions of *Drop Seoi-nage* in terms of the different directions for the orthodox *Tomoe-nage* and the *Yoko-tomoe-nage*. In a way, the *Drop Seoi* is like a sacrifice throw, but from a different position.

Grips

In the *Drop Seoi-nages* described later in this section you will find both orthodox and unorthodox techniques, but the fundamental difference in opportunity between *Morote* and *Ippon* is best dealt with here. The distinction is very simple.

The opportunity for *Ippon-seoi-nage* usually comes when the gripping is still unsettled. In the in-fighting for the superior grip it is possible suddenly to take an *Ippon-seoi* hold, twist and drop and catch the opponent completely unawares. It is difficult for an *Ippon-seoi* to be effected when the grips are established, because the opponent's arms too often prove an impenetrable barrier.

A settled grip, however, provides the opportunity for a *Morote-seoi*, provided the attacker has achieved her favourite grip, is able to manoeuvre her opponent into position, and can negate the defences.

Conclusion

The importance of the *Drop Seoi-nage* in women's judo makes it imperative that every woman studies the technique. Each should have at least one version in her repertoire, no matter what her weight category – though the lighter weights will inevitably depend more on speed for success, while the heavier weights will rely more on top control. Even women who show no interest or aptitude for the technique should spend some time learning its intricacies, for there is no doubt that during every randori and every contest it will be used to attack at least once, if not more.

Morote-seoi-nage
(double hand shoulder throw)

Introduction

The basic hand action of the *Morote-seoi* is the same whether the intention is to execute a *Drop Morote* or a standing throw, although, as we have said, it is the *Drop Seoi* that works when the standard of the participants is more or less the same. Perhaps *Drop Morote-seoi-nage* is attempted more by women than by men because the greater range of movement women possess in their elbows (due to their lack of heavily-muscled arms and shoulders) makes them more capable of 'slipping' defences. This is generally a throw for middle-weights and below.

Basic Technique

The throw itself comes from the accuracy and speed with which the left leg (in a right-handed technique) makes its half-circle swing. The hands control, but if the surprise element is maintained everything depends on that turning action. It must, therefore, be given much attention in training.

Important Points

1. The main problem with the hands is to get the right elbow across. Uke will be working to nullify the threat from that right elbow, but there are a couple of tricks tori can use to free it. The first is to take the right elbow sharply up, which weakens uke's control. The second is to take a low lapel grip with the right hand and, when uke tries to control the arm, move it sharply to the right before switching it back in and across uke's chest into the throwing position. This is particularly useful when uke has the inside grip.
2. Once again, the best time for the attack is when on the move.
3. The throw is greatly improved when the rotation action is increased. This is achieved by pushing off with the legs as shown in the illustration. This is particularly necessary when the throwing direction is to the right.

Tip

Ensure that the right wrist is turned well in. Injuries to both wrist and elbows are caused by *Morote* actions which are unsuccessful. If uke pulls back to defend, tori's right wrist will be badly bent back. If the wrist is turned, it not only raises the potential success rate but prevents injury if the rest of the movement is sloppy.

Double Lapel Drop Seoi-nage

Introduction

The beauty of the double lapel grip is that you can attack equally well on either side, although uke's grip has to be taken into consideration. The weakness is that unless the direction is directly over the top, or the power of the throw very great indeed, uke can prevent or at least lessen the score by putting her hands down.

Basic Technique

The double lapel grip has the advantage of giving uke a good defence, because it effectively controls the space between the two participants. A fluid, half-circle swing is essential, otherwise uke can use her hands to create space and step off the technique.

Important Points

1. This technique does require a fair amount of upper body strength and is thus perhaps more useful for heavier women and women who have worked weights.
2. The throw must be straight over the top – even if uke gets her hands down to the mat, she will still not be able to prevent herself being thrown.

Tip

This works well from a jigotai situation. With the double lapel, tori pulls down uke's head, then suddenly releases the tension while maintaining the control. As uke's head comes up, so tori drops in for the throw.

Eri-seoi-nage
(lapel shoulder throw)

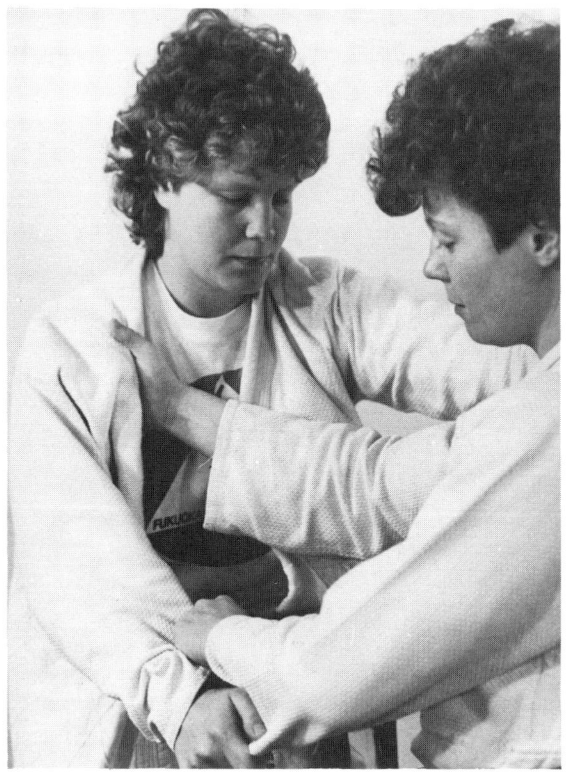

Introduction

This, like the *Ippon-seoi-nage* techniques, works best from a grip-fighting situation, although it can also work from a relatively static position because the rapid change of grip inevitably causes its own movement. Moreover, it works equally well for all sizes, for it can be performed fairly slowly and does not necessarily require great flexibility. When it works, it is one of the most spectacular techniques used by women.

Basic Technique

As uke reaches for her lapel grip, tori takes the cross lapel grip first. She then has a choice of taking either the sleeve or the same lapel as she makes the full entry. After this the action is basically a *Morote-seoi-nage*, possibly dropping on to the right knee only.

Example of the double lapel same side grip.

Important Point

In competition tori can only hold with two hands on one side of the jacket while making an attack; this emphasises the importance of crisp action throughout.

Tip

This works particularly well if, in a right-handed attack, uke is caught while moving to her left, which means she is caught on tori's back. If uke is moving towards her right, an overemphasised twist in the drop is required so that uke effectively runs on to the technique.

Morote-seoi-nage-makikomi
(shoulder throw with winding movement)

1982 World Championships: Loretta Doyle of Great Britain attacks Edith Hrovat of Austria with a Drop Seoi-nage.

This shows the 'drop' version.

Introduction

This is an unusual variation of a classic throw which will not please traditionalists – but it works. At first I noticed it happening by accident, then I gradually developed its technical base. It is a useful trick for all *Seoi-nage* exponents, including, surprisingly, heavyweights, because it simply evades the strong-arm defence that stops most *Seoi-nages* before they can begin.

Basic Technique

Tori feels the strong lapel grip of the opponent boring into her shoulder. She takes an unusually low lapel grip to give her plenty of cloth with which to manoeuvre. She brings the fist high and by rotating with her whole body allows her elbow to pass over the opponent's defensive arm. A further rotation, combined with a winding movement down to the ground, completes the technique.

Important Points

1. The turning movement should be executed by tori stepping across uke with her right leg, not by bringing her left leg round in a half-circle.
2. The elbow should be brought across over uke's forearm or wrist, not higher up. It must then clamp on using the armpit. This allows more room for rotation.

Tip

Uchikomi can initially be executed without the *Makikomi* to finish the throw. There is no reason why this 'elbow over' *Seoi-nage* cannot work from a standing position, but in competition it generally concludes with a *Makikomi*.

Drop Ippon-seoi-nage
(one arm shoulder throw)

Introduction

It is now no longer possible to achieve an *Ippon-seoi-nage* against reasonable opposition using a sleeve grip. I wonder if this was ever possible. Yet *Ippon-seoi* is still taught with the sleeve grip, rather than the collar grip. Traditions, even when they are obsolete, survive. *Drop Ippon-seoi* is probably the most frequently used single technique in women's judo, yet the function of that collar grip must be more widely understood.

Basic Technique

Tori's left hand takes a collar grip over uke's right arm and, with a left-leg swing, drops and throws.

Important Points

1. Tori's left hand must go over uke's right arm because this enables her to 'lock on' to uke's defending arm. Uke's forearm is clamped against tori's chest, so she cannot pull back to escape or counter but finds herself caught in the whirl of the turn and drop.
2. The throw to the side has a higher success rate than the throw over the top.

Tip

Tori must turn in for the throw before uke can grasp with two hands. A two-handed grip by uke can make the throw very difficult to achieve.

Opposite: Example of the grip.

Ippon-seoi-nage Arm Trap

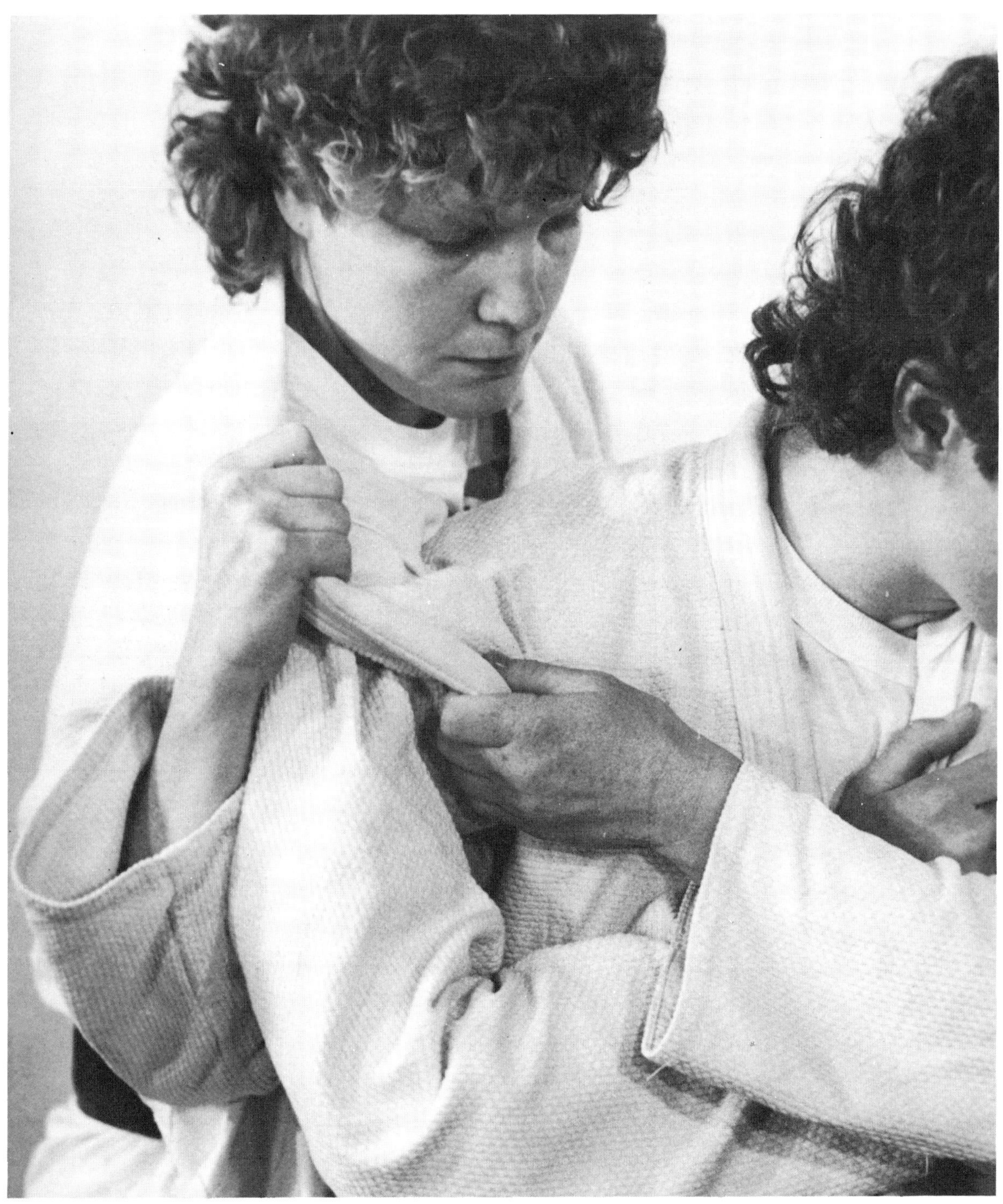

Introduction

This is a small variation, but a useful addition to *Ippon-seoi-nage* specialists of all weights. It can be extremely disconcerting for uke.

Basic Technique

Tori's left arm takes uke's right lapel in the normal manner, but then feeds it over uke's arm. Tori's right arm then comes under the arm, picks up the lapel, and tightens it firmly around uke's arm, before dropping with the half-circle leg swing.

Important Point

Although this may feel odd at the beginning it is actually a very strong position for tori, as the control of uke's arm is so good that a natural defence is created.

Biceps Seoi-otoshi
(drop shoulder throw)

Introduction

This is a useful technique against an opponent with an extreme stance, as it deals directly with the main means of defence – the lapel grip. It works particularly well for middleweights and above as it can be executed at a relatively slow pace.

Basic Technique

Facing an extreme right-handed player, tori takes hold of uke's sleeve by the bicep with her right hand first, with the left hand then taking hold of uke's sleeve. Tori can now either step across and take the throw in a classic *Seoi-otoshi* manner or, using the half-circle swing of the left leg, drop on to the left knee.

Important Points

1. The entry is made considerably easier if the right hand can bend uke's elbow a little.
2. When tori rotates, the body contact should be firm. It is crucial to use the hips well to maintain a good body line.

Tip

Get as close as you can with the sideways stance at the beginning while maintaining a reasonable defence, although it is the surprise from the unorthodox nature of the grips that is one of the strongest elements of the throw.

ASHIWAZA

Kouchi-gari Ouchi-gari De-ashi-barai Kosoto-gari Kouchi-gake Ouchi-gake Sasae-tsuri-komi-ashi

Introduction

Ashiwaza occupies a somewhat ambivalent place among judo techniques. A good foot sweep is widely regarded as an immensely skilful achievement, yet there is a prevailing feeling of an ashiwaza being a nifty trick. To lose to a good *Drop Seoi-nage* is a straightforward defeat, but to lose to a clean foot sweep is often regarded as unlucky, rather like slipping on a banana skin. Yet ashiwaza is one of the richest veins of judo technique, with a range and a variety that certainly equal any of the other major categories, including shoulder and hip throw. Its reliance on good movement, fast feet, technical accomplishment and timing, rather than explosive upper body strength, indicates that ashiwaza has an enormous amount to offer women's judo.

When ashiwaza is discussed the immediate image is of *Okuri-ashi-barai*, one of the most outstanding throws of the Gokyo. It is rarely seen in top competition, because it is a difficult throw to execute as a direct attack against a highly skilled opponent. However, it remains the epitome of ashiwaza, because it appears both spectacular and effortless.

Okuri-ashi-barai and its closely related throw *De-ashi-barai* are only one kind of ashiwaza – one that relies on a sweeping action across the body. There are numerous other kinds of ashiwaza utilising different actions, taking uke's feet in different directions, with varying kinds of upper body control. There are the *Kouchi* and the *Tsuri-komi-ashi* throws, which vary from strong sweeping actions to simple blocks, and *Kosoto-gari* and *Kosoto-gake* which have similar variations.

Ashiwaza can be devastating as direct attacks, or 'openers', to break through very rigid defences; they can be equally effective as 'finishers', as the final *coup de grâce* in a string of combinations. If an opponent is softened up with a barrage of attacks from hip or shoulder throws, it is surprising how susceptible she can be to a small foot clip.

This is particularly true where the randori or competition has developed into the tug of war. When opponents close, the grips usually dominate the attention. The complex in-fighting as one strives to achieve the required hold while preventing her opponent from taking any advantage diverts much of the awareness away from the feet, and from this an ashiwaza, unseen and unexpected, can come as a complete surprise.

When well executed, the ashiwaza seems to come from nowhere, and, moreover, it can come from left or right. The relatively small body movement required means that ashiwaza can be effectively used by all women, although most will find a natural predilection for specific kinds rather than regularly using a wide selection.

It is also important because it is one of the few classes of judo throws where a minimal body commitment is required. You can make

Opposite: Nakahara of Japan throws Madjan of Poland with Kouchi-gari.

CHINES À ÉCRIR
DE BUREAU

a strong ashiwaza attack, but a mistake need not be irrevocable.

Basic Technique

There are two basic kinds of ashiwaza. The first requires tori to hold uke's body still momentarily to allow the feet to be swept from under her. Into this category fall *Okuri-ashi-barai*, *De-ashi-barai*, *Kouchi-gari*, *Ouchi-gari*, *Kosoto-gari* and *Harai-tsuri-komi-ashi*. These techniques mainly emerge from smooth, moving situations. Uke feels as if she has been caught in the air.

In the second kind, tori blocks or hooks with the foot and then moves the body over the trapped leg. Into this category fall *Kosoto-gake*, *Yoko-gake*, *Kouchi-gake*, *Ouchi-gake*, *Hiza-guruma* and *Sasae-tsuri-komi-ashi*. These generally emerge from a static situation, although when they can be performed on the move the results can be very dramatic indeed.

In both categories, opportunities for variations within the throws are numerous. For example, the success or failure of a *Kouchi-gari* may depend not only on the correct timing and movement of tori, but also on the direction of the sweep. Perhaps a classic sweep is required, where tori's foot catches uke behind the heel and sweeps her in the direction of her toes. Perhaps a slight resistance on uke's part requires a different direction from tori, taking the opponent's foot more to the side. Or a switch from one to the other may be called for – a failed attempt at a sweep may indicate that the opponent is vulnerable to a blocking or hooking ashiwaza.

A quick woman, with natural feeling for movement, may feel more comfortable with the sweeping aspects of ashiwaza. A larger, stronger woman will inevitably find blocking or hooking ashiwaza easier – although which is appropriate depends to a certain extent on the opponent. On the whole, a firm, upright posture is required for those specialising in sweeping ashiwaza, while a more varied posture is possible for those who feel more comfortable with blocking ashiwaza.

All women should be conversant with both kinds of ashiwaza, even if they specialise in one, and ashiwaza should be regarded by all women as a major area of judo study.

Important Points

Many people remark that ashiwaza – especially the *Ashi-barai* – is a technique that comes spontaneously and naturally to the exponent. How often does one see ashiwaza uchikomi, for instance? However, ashiwaza can be developed in a systematic way just the same as any other throw.

Start with the practice of turning the sole of the foot (this not only prevents painful kicking, but gives tori greater control) and moving around the mat with a sweeping action. This is one of the practices in judo that you can usefully do on your own; only in the next stage, when ashiwaza movement feels smooth, is a partner necessary.

General movement, as well as the basic sweeping or blocking motion, can be developed in solitary practice. If sweeping ashiwaza is difficult to use against a static opponent, methods must be developed to make that opponent move – and perhaps the easiest way is to move yourself. Movement patterns culminating in ashiwaza can be developed, which later will probably change into more spontaneous actions, incorporating the more unpredictable reactions of a stiff opponent. Although some opponents seem unmovable, few are able to resist quite lively movements from their partners. They will move, if only to come square again to their partners. It is during this movement that an ashiwaza can be skilfully slipped in.

It should also be noted that ashiwaza can serve its mistress throughout her judo career. A quicksilver *Kouchi-gari* can be used to good effect throughout a top contest career and, twenty years later, that woman can still be using her feet to surprise the younger contest women of the day, but with a more canny blocking *Kouchi-gake* that just traps the foot and enables her to tip her surprised opponent backwards.

Tip

Very few people, men or women, are invulnerable to ashiwaza. The only question really is to which ashiwaza are they most vulnerable?

Kouchi-gari
(minor inner reap)

Introduction

The classic *Kouchi-gari* works as well for women as it does for men, and for women of all weight categories. The opportunity presents itself both when uke is in an upright posture and when she is leaning backwards.

Basic Technique

The principle is for the arms to pull the opponent on to the leg which is to be reaped. The true *Kouchi-gari* makes uke feel that she has just stepped on to a banana skin. Although it can work against a static opponent, it is best executed on the move when uke will be less stable.

Important Points

1. In the *Gari* techniques, the working leg is the reaping leg – an obvious point which is, nevertheless, important when comparing the *Kouchi-gari* with the *Kouchi-gake*. The reaping foot takes away the advanced foot of uke as tori bears the weight of both bodies down on to the spot where uke intended to step.
2. Tori must have firm control of uke's weight, particularly with the lapel arm.

Tip

Tori can help to prevent uke stepping off a *Kouchi-gari* by holding the sleeve grip on the side of the elbow; as tori's foot comes across to reap, so the left hand pushes uke's elbow across the body. Effective uchikomi can be done to develop this movement.

Ouchi-gari
(major inner reap)

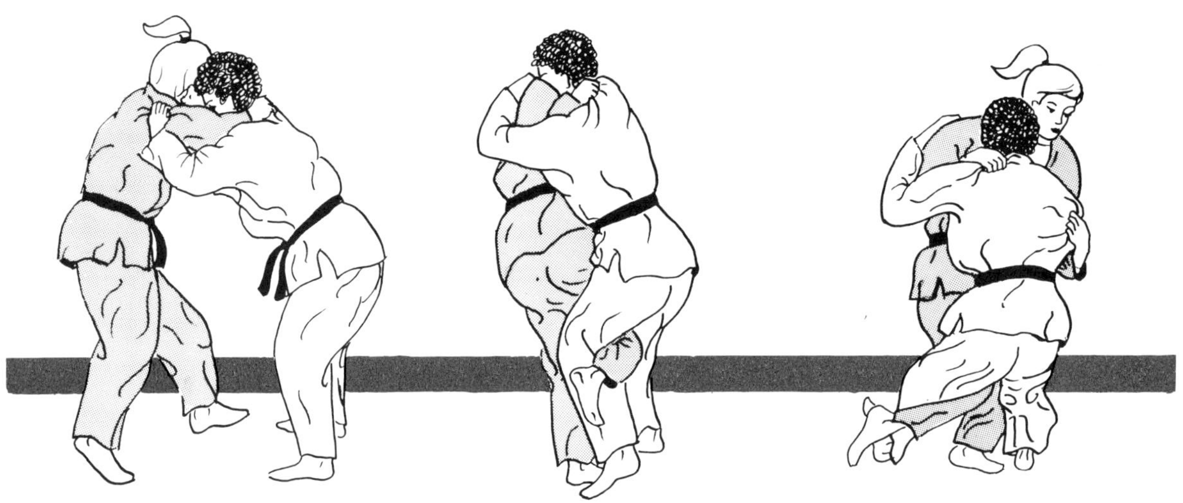

1984 British Open Championships: Robin Chapman of the United States scores with Ouchi-gari.

Introduction

In its classic form this throw is seen in all weight categories. Once again, however, in women's judo movement is the key, and if the situation is not a moving one then movement must be created.

To execute an *Ouchi-gari*, uke should be in the standard jigotai position or at least be pulling backwards to check forward impetus.

Basic Technique

With a standard grip, tori creates movement by stepping across her opponent using the lapel grip to pull uke in a half-circle behind them. This half-circle is then accentuated by tori's reaping leg. The combination of the pull and the reap that continues it takes uke down.

Important Points

1. The hands are a crucial element of the throw. Constant hand control is required, particularly the lapel grip which should be pulling with a slightly downwards action to ensure that uke cannot step off the throw.
2. The working leg is the reaping leg. The other leg is important only for positioning.
3. Tori must ensure that her head turns well towards her lapel grip and the back corner where uke is being thrown. If the head is not turned correctly, the throw will fail and tori will be left wide open to a counter *Kosoto-gari*. However, do not take the head past the lapel grip or control can be lost.

1984 World Championships: Loretta Doyle of Great Britain attacks with Ouchi-gari.

Tip

Although this is a throw to the rear corner, do not think of pushing at any point. When the time comes to finish the technique you will push automatically. If you think of pushing too early, you will simply push uke away from your throw.

De-ashi-barai
(advanced foot sweep)

Introduction

This is traditionally taught as advancing foot sweep, but it is technically extremely difficult to time the throw so perfectly to catch uke as her foot is coming forwards and as her weight is being transferred. This basic throw still works at top levels, but as the opponent is moving backwards or sideways. In this form it is useful for all weight categories.

Basic Technique

As uke steps backwards, tori sweeps the leading foot just as the weight is being taken off it. The hands stop the upper body and, as the foot is being swept across, direct uke's weight down to the spot where her foot had been a moment before.

Important Points

1. A sleeve and lapel grip is necessary for good control of uke's upper body – hand control is at least half of this throw. A double lapel grip does not give sufficient directional control.
2. It is possible to sweep in either direction from one sleeve and lapel grip.
3. The sweeping foot should ideally be straight to inject full power into the throw, and the sole of the foot should be turned for optimum directional control.

Tip

Although this is described as an advanced foot sweep, it can also be used when uke is coming across, for instance for a *Tai-otoshi* or a *Kouchi-gari*. Speed allied to control is essential.

Kosoto-gari as a direct attack
(minor outer reap)

1983 British Open Championships: Shigemoto of the United States scores with Kosoto-gari *to win the over 72 kilos gold medal.*

Introduction

Although this works most frequently from a combination situation, it is also possible to use it against an opponent who has a sideways stance. This technique is generally of most use to middle and heavyweights, for the lightweights are often too sharp to be caught by it.

Basic Technique

There are two kinds of *Kosoto-gari*. The first is a fairly dynamic attack, with tori bearing uke's weight down on the foot and then reaping it strongly. The second is a kind of multiple attack, or 'sticky foot' *Kosoto-gari*, in which tori tips her opponent on to one heel with quite subtle hand control and then blocks that heel with the sole of her foot. By pushing off her back leg, tori manages to unsettle uke further; uke finds herself being driven backwards until, with a final reap, she is thrown.

Important Points

1. In the first kind of *Kosoto-gari* tori uses her sole or calf to reap, while in the second only the sole (the foot must be turned well) is used.
2. Although the distinction between *Gari* throws and *Gake* throws is generally quite clear (in the first the reaping foot is the 'working' foot; in the second the back foot is the 'working' foot), the 'sticky foot' *Kosoto-gari* is an exception. In this both legs are working equally, right up to the final moment of the throw.

Tip

What begins as a *Kosoto-gari* can end up very effectively as *Nidan-kosoto-gari*, where the reaping leg takes uke's far leg; or even as *Tani-otoshi*, where suddenly a 'sacrifice' element is introduced into the action.

Kouchi-gake
(minor inner hook)

Introduction

This 'hooking' version of *Kouchi* is technically easier to accomplish than the classic *Gari* or reaping version, because it does not require such fine hand control and timing. That is one reason why it has a higher scoring rate in contests. It is effective for women of all sizes, particularly when performed with the leg grab as an additional factor in preventing uke from avoiding it.

The opportunity is signalled by a strongly defensive posture, when uke is clearly concerned about a throw to the front.

Basic Technique

The whole feeling of the *Kouchi-gake* attack is different to that of the *Kouchi-gari*. *Kouchi-gake* feels like the fencer's lunge; it is a direct, simple attack with total commitment. The hand comes down to pick up the hooked leg just to ensure that there is no possible escape for uke.

Important Points

1. As in all *Gake* throws it is the back leg, not the hooking leg, that does most of the work. The front leg just hooks, while the back leg pushes off firmly to launch the total weight of tori at uke.
2. In the initial attack it is extremely important for tori to pull uke on to her, both with the lapel hand and the sleeve hand, and not to push. If you push, you are likely to push your opponent away from you, not bring her on to the throw.

Tip

This is technically a direct attack, but it is possible to think of it as a combination in that uke must be set up by two or three strong attacks to the front, after which it is possible to unleash the *Kouchi-gake*. It is also effective at the start of a contest when both partners are likely to be defensive and cautious. It has the advantage of being a throw which it is almost impossible to counter.

1984 World Championships: Kouchi-gake *by Marie-France Colignon of France.*

Ouchi-gake
(major inner reap)

Introduction

Ouchi-gake is mainly used by lightweights and middleweights and, like its sister throw *Kouchi-gake*, relies on a totally committed attack in the form of a fencing lunge. The speed into the throw and the momentum created by tori's body can bring success to the throw despite a lack of hand control. This is shown here by the additional factor of the leg grab which prevents uke stepping off the technique.

Basic Technique

Tori takes a normal grip except that the right hand is best placed on the outside of uke's arm to facilitate a swift movement for the leg grab. Tori lunges into position, hooks the leg and immediately drops her hand to pick up the leg. By dropping her body weight on to her knee tori effectively keeps uke on her heels, even though she no longer has control of uke's left shoulder. Also, by aiming eventually to land on her knee tori's initial attack will definitely be low. The direction of the attack is directly backwards.

Important Points

1. The back leg is the main working leg in this technique. The forward leg just hooks, but the back leg drives hard once the hook has been achieved.
2. Tori's head should be turned either to face uke's chest or even past uke's left side in order to ensure correct positioning of the body.

Tip

The opportunity for *Ouchi-gake*, like its sister throw, arises with a strongly defensive opponent, but the throw can be set up by some determined, but safe forward attacks. *Ouchi-gake* is also a throw that works well for women from a static situation.

1986 European Championships: Karen Briggs of Great Britain attacks Loly Veguillas of Spain during their under 48 kilos final, won by Briggs.

Sasae-tsuri-komi-ashi
(propping drawing ankle throw)

Introduction

This technique is more commonly used by middleweights because it generally emerges from a fairly static situation. However, speed of movement by tori can often compensate for lack of arm and shoulder strength. In fact, this throw is all about rotation: the more determined the rotational attack, the better the throw.

Basic Technique

Sasae-tsuri-komi-ashi (propping drawing ankle) is traditionally taught as a right-handed attack from a right-handed grip. However, women use it more frequently as a left-handed attack from a right-handed grip, with the element of surprise proving one of the strong points of the technique.

Important Points

1. The right hand grip should be high on the collar so that tori can control uke's head. Head control is crucial. *Tsuri* comes from the Japanese word meaning 'to fish', and the best results are obtained when there is a slight lifting action from the right collar grip in addition to the rotation.
2. Tori uses her left sleeve grip to force uke's right arm backwards in order to unsettle further uke's balance.
3. The blocking foot must connect with uke's shin when uke's left foot is back. It can be done with other timings, but the most unbalancing effect comes when uke is forced to lean 'into space' by tori's fast rotation. The control of the head with the high collar grip effectively prevents uke putting her left foot forward to regain her balance.

Tip

This can work spectacularly when it is slipped in as a sudden change from a series of strong right-handed attacks such as *Uchimata* or *Koshi-guruma*.

1984 World Championships:
Margaret Castro of the United States.

TOMOE-NAGE

Tomoe-nage Tomoe-nage variation
Yoko-tomoe-nage

Tomoe-nage
(circle throw)

Introduction

This is one of the best known of all the classic judo throws, both inside and outside judo circles, yet it remains a high scorer in women's judo. Any study of sacrifice throws must begin here, for unless the basic principles have been understood from the orthodox *Tomoe-nage* the variations and combinations that are always being devised will not have a reliable foundation.

Basic Technique

Tomoe-nage can be executed from either a conventional sleeve and lapel grip or a double lapel grip, but the principle remains the same. An opposite force is created, with the arms pulling and the foot pushing. The double lapel offers a more powerful contrary motion and has the element of surprise, whereas the sleeve and lapel offers better directional control. *Tomoe-nage* exponents must take their pick – or learn to do both. What cannot be skimped is the basic stepping action, where first the standing leg is placed between the opponent's legs and then the other foot is placed in the stomach. The failure of *Tomoe-nage* attempts is usually because this first step is omitted.

The opportunity for this throw arises when uke has a bent posture and, preferably, is pushing slightly.

Important Points

1. The throwing leg should not be straightened too early or it will just push uke away. Uke must be nicely balanced before she is flipped over the top.
2. The entry and throw must be as fast as possible. It is a weakness of the orthodox *Tomoe-nage* that uke is a long time in the air – and the standard of spatial awareness in top judo competitors now is high. Unless the throw is fast or the hand control extremely good, a reasonable opponent will spin out.

Tips

When practising, it is useful to follow right the way through in a backwards roll to achieve the full potential of the throw. If, in contest or randori, tori's hips do not come off the ground the full action, and perhaps the ippon, is lost.

The best timing for *Tomoe-nage* is, in a right-handed throw, when the opponent's left leg is slightly advanced. Tori then swiftly steps in deeply with her left leg and makes the throw with her right leg.

Tomoe-nagc Variation

Introduction

This variation elegantly illustrates the dynamic nature of judo – how it has continued to develop to meet and overcome defences. Over the years men and women learned to block the traditional *Tomoe-nage* by dropping their hips and putting their weight on the right leg (in a right-handed attack). So this change of direction evolved.

Basic Technique

Tori comes in for a traditional *Tomoe-nage* and, when she feels resistance to the 'straight over the top' motion, uses her foot and sleeve grip to take uke to her left.

Important Points

1. Tori's foot must follow uke right down to the mat, thus enabling tori to come up immediately into groundwork.
2. This is not a direct attack. The attack has started as a traditional *Tomoe-nage* and only changed because of uke's defence.

Tip

Only training in both the traditional *Tomoe-nage* and the following *Yoko-tomoe-nage* will instil within tori the instinctive reaction that this variation requires. It is generally not possible to predict; it is simply felt in mid-throw.

Opposite: 1982 World Championships: Karen Briggs of Great Britain throws her Japanese opponent with Tomoe-nage *for ippon on her way to winning her first under 48 kilos gold medal.*

LONG
WAZA-ARI
KEIK
YUKO
CH
SHI

Yoko-tomoe-nage
(side and circle throw)

Normal side entry.

Direction three.

Introduction

This is another development from the traditional *Tomoe-nage*. The 'side' element of this throw is established by tori's initial movement rather than necessarily by the direction of the throw, although that can add an even more confusing element for uke. Like all *Tomoe-nages*, the signal for the opportunity is uke's bent posture. It is generally useful for competitors up to light middleweights (61 kilos) because of the flexibility required in the entry. It works best from a moving situation, but it can also work from the static position.

Basic Technique

From a conventional right-handed sleeve and collar grip, tori watches for uke's left leg to go back. Tori then twists to her right, taking her head down to uke's left foot. Uke may have been expecting a traditional *Tomoe-nage* and felt confident that she could block it, but this surprise change of direction completely unsettles her balance and she is pulled round with tori's right leg already in position. Tori can then throw in a number of directions according to uke's reaction, but generally it is straight over the top of her head.

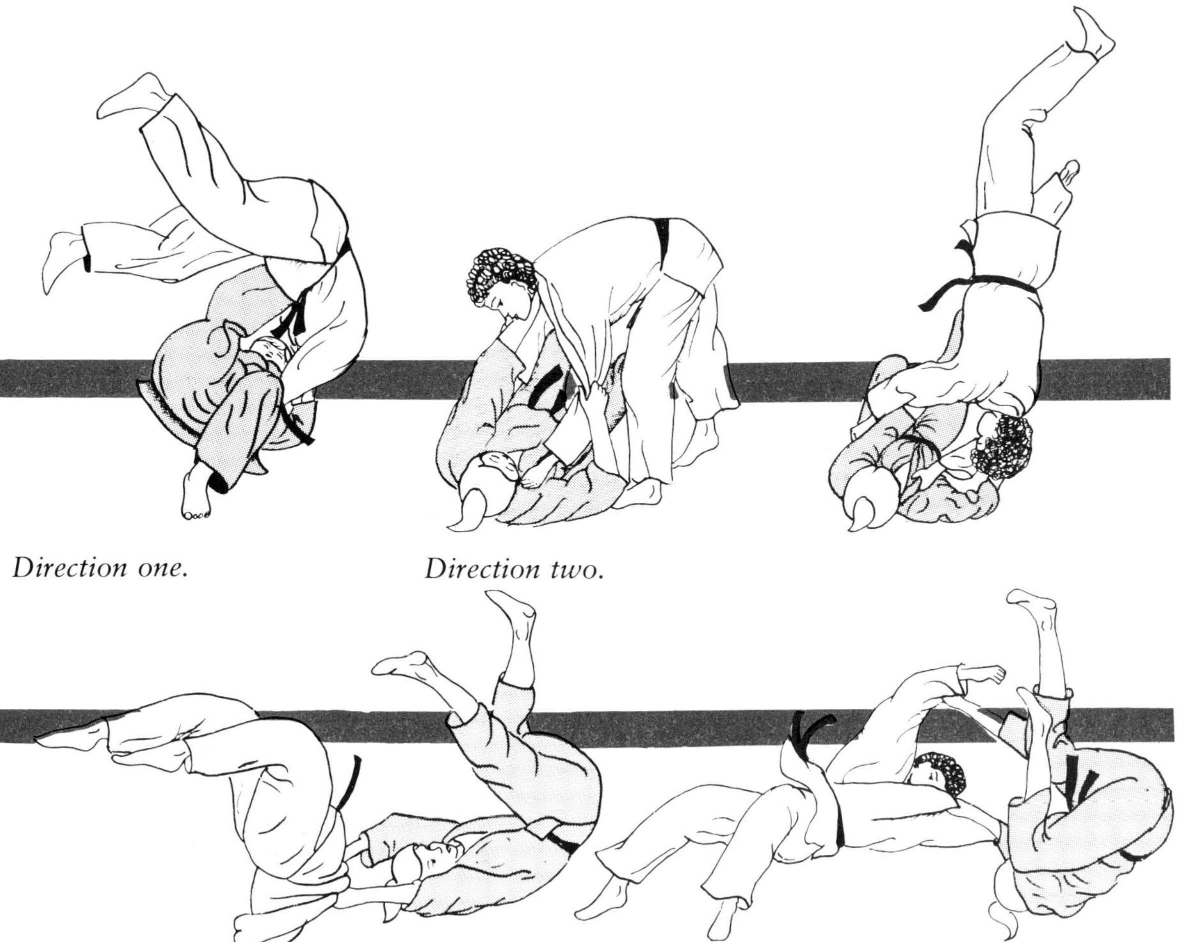

Direction one.

Direction two.

Important Points

1. This *Yoko-tomoe-nage* significantly cuts down the time that uke spends in the air, confuses the opponent, and thus increases the chances of success.
2. Tori must train to take the opponent in all three possible directions, starting with over the top, then to the left and to the right. Surround tori with crash mats, feed her ukes, and make her throw in the three directions.
3. As in all *Tomoe-nages*, do not straighten the throwing leg too early – before uke is off her feet and balanced on the bent throwing leg.

Tips

This *Yoko-tomoe-nage* can work spectacularly when uke is persuaded to pull back her left leg sharply following a series of strong *Ouchi-gari* attacks. As uke snatches her left foot back to avoid an *Ouchi-gari*, tori can slip in neatly for *Yoko-tomoe*.

Another *Yoko-tomoe* uses the leg on the same side as the sleeve grip. If tori's right hand holds uke's sleeve, then her head goes down to uke's left foot and tori's right leg goes into the stomach. The throwing direction is to the right of tori, and can be especially effective against a defensive uke.

HIP TECHNIQUES

Ogoshi Uki-goshi Tsuri-goshi
Sode-tsure-komi-goshi Oguruma

Ogoshi
(major hip throw)

Introduction

The traditional *Ogoshi* is rarely seen in men's judo, but remains a very effective throw for women. This may be partly because women have greater flexibility in their hips, and partly because women do not have the muscular power to break the grip once the arm is around the back, which for men is an easier task. The *Ogoshi* is particularly useful for women in the heavier weight categories; lighter women can avoid the throw with their swift movements.

Basic Technique

The secret of the success of *Ogoshi* lies in the powerful opposite effect of the arm behind the back pulling and the hip coming across. Curiously, it is usually possible to get the arm around the back (it should go as far as is comfortable), particularly with an opponent who maintains a sideways stance. With practice, and with the acquisition of a few gripping tricks, it is possible even against an opponent who stands square.

Important Points

1. An ippon score is more likely when a sleeve grip is obtained, although it is also possible to throw well with a lapel grip so long as the hip is brought through further to lift the opponent clear of the ground, preventing the free hand from making contact.
2. On the initial contact if the opponent resists, a slight bend of the legs allows tori to regain control and spin uke over.

Tip

The strongest hold around the back is on the belt, but this is not always possible and a secure grip on the back of the judogi can suffice.

Uki-goshi
(floating hip)

Introduction

My study of *Nage-no-kata* made me realise just how useful this throw can be. Shorter women were frequently finding that their heads were being pulled down by the collar grips of taller opponents; *Nage-no-kata*, I discovered, had an answer.

Basic Technique

As a tall opponent reaches forwards to take a high grip, tori instantaneously slips in an *Uki-goshi*, the arm going around the back.

Important Points

1. This is a reaction throw – the attack must be immediate.
2. Despite this, tori must prepare for the throw by ensuring that she takes her lapel grip first – on the opposite side of uke's anticipated lapel grip.
3. *Uki-goshi* works well from a final standing position, but the sudden drop to the knees can come as another complete surprise.

Tip

Tori must obtain her own lapel grip but stay away from uke's arm until she is ready. Then she can subtly 'give' uke her shoulder for the collar grip, before darting inside.

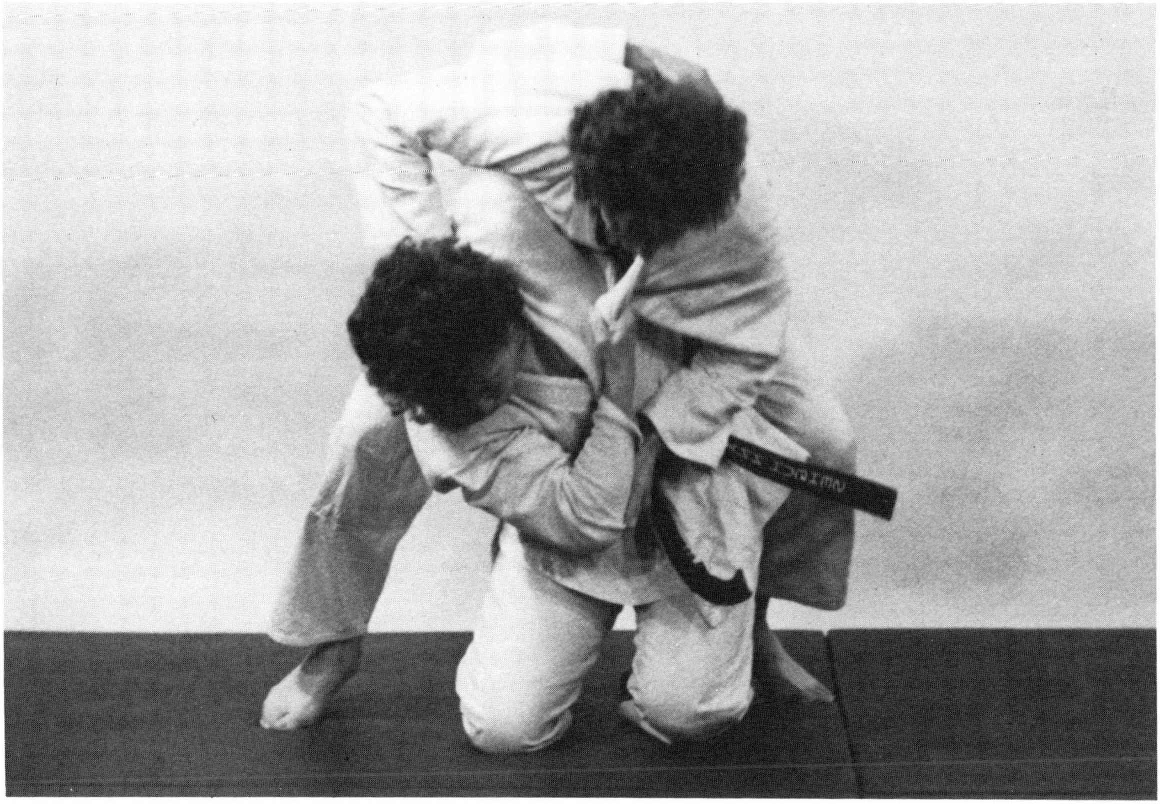

Tsuri-goshi
(lift-hip throw)

Introduction

The traditional form of *Tsuri-goshi* requires a considerable amount of lifting strength which is rarely available to women. A variation of the original technique, however, has proved effective at the top level of competition, largely because it is based on rotation rather than a power lift. The opportunity arises when uke is in a bent posture.

Basic Technique

In the traditional form, tori's right hand (in a right-handed attack) reaches over uke's left shoulder to take the belt. But at this point, either tori's right hand picks up the belt on the other (right) side, or, tori having taken the belt by going over the left shoulder, uke ducks under the arm. This is the situation tori was looking for. She now clamps her opponent to her body, rather than attempting to lift, and, stepping across, rotates swiftly and strongly. It is also possible simply to turn on the balls of the feet.

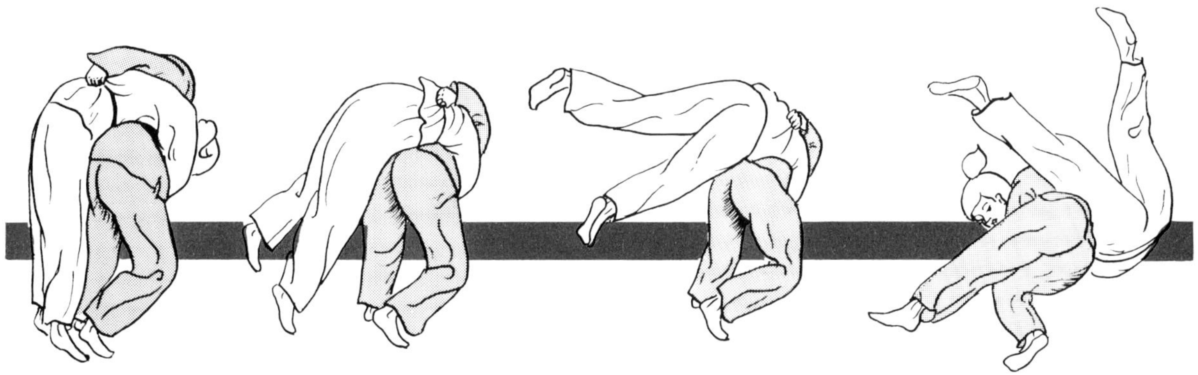

Important Points

1. It is the rotation that takes uke off her feet and straight down to the ground.
2. Once the right arm has clamped, it must not be loosened. Any gaps that appear will possibly prevent the throw, or the control in *Newaza*, or both.

Tip

It is possible to execute the *Tsuri-goshi* by taking the opponent's judogi at shoulder-blade level, but the belt grip is stronger.

Opposite: Heather Ford of Great Britain attacks Lieckens of Belgium with Tsuri-goshi.

Sode-tsuri-komi-goshi
(sleeve lift pull hip throw)

Introduction

The strength of this throw in both men's and women's judo lies in the fact that it is a left-handed throw from a right-handed grip, or vice versa, which confuses opponents. Women have had to develop a slightly different style because the traditional attack requires a powerful lifting action from the sleeve grip. Once practised, *Sode-tsuri* becomes an excellent contest and randori technique for women of generally middleweight and below, although heavier women with good hip actions will also find it useful.

Basic Technique

With a right-handed grip, tori's left hand takes normal sleeve grip. Men have the power to lift the arm here, but women should just use the left hand to stabilise uke's right arm. With uke's upper body fixed, tori can shoot the hip across and turn uke over.

Important Points

1. It is best to make the attack before uke has settled into a strong defensive posture, otherwise she becomes more difficult to turn.
2. It is crucial to move the hip well across to catch uke. Even when the throw works well, it is generally a *yuko* throw or *waza-ari* throw because uke often manages to get her left hand down to the floor. The better the hip movement, the better the result.
3. Most women will find it more effective to avoid attempting to lift the opponent and simply rely on the drop. However, it is feasible for women to do this as a standing technique, so long as there is a strong surprise element.

Tip

To confuse the opponent even further, it is worth developing a right *Makikomi* in conjunction with *Sode-tsuri-komi-goshi*. A slight feint for *Sode-tsuri*, particularly after a real attempt has been made, renders uke extremely susceptible to a strong change to right *Makikomi*.

Oguruma
(major wheel)

Introduction

This elegant and powerful throw seems to be the preserve of the middleweights, who have just the right combination of speed, weight and strength.

Basic Technique

Movement is the core of this throw. The opponent must be moving sideways or in a half-circle towards tori's right side. This allows tori to spin across with the right foot.

Important Points

1. *Oguruma* can only be developed into a major technique by women if they practise it on the move, for it is only when the opponent's momentum is really committed can the 'big wheel' be set in motion.
2. Traditional instruction insists that tori's leg goes high up at uke's waist level, but this is impractical. Tori must place her leg across uke's loins and right thigh, then her arms can wheel uke over, and tori's body rotates.

Tip

The smooth wheeling motion can only be achieved if tori's arms are relatively free. A loose sleeve and lapel grip is needed – not so loose that uke's upper body cannot be controlled, but not so stiff that all the spring and elasticity in tori's arms are lost.

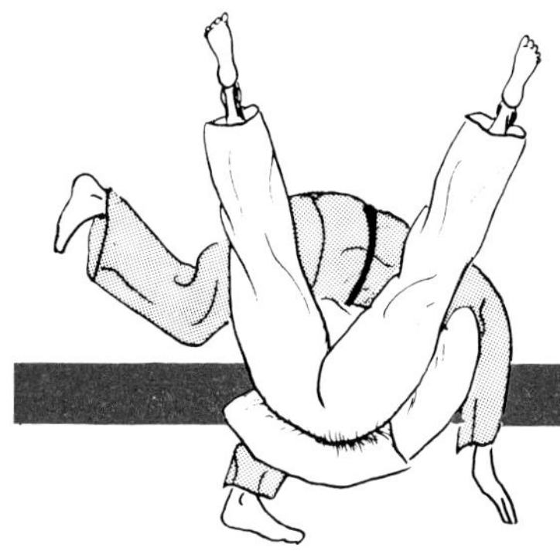

TAI-OTOSHI

Tai-otoshi   Wrong Leg Tai-otoshi   Hikki-otoshi

Tai-otoshi
(body drop)

Introduction

This is the classic *Tai-otoshi* which is used by all weight categories. In women's judo it usually requires movement to work well, so the timing of the throw must be perfect.

Basic Technique

Tori must get uke moving in a half-circle on to tori's sleeve grip, so that as tori's right leg comes across to trip uke, uke's impetus is already beyond the point of no return. A static *Tai-otoshi* for women is only feasible when, in a right-handed attack, uke's right leg is back, so that the throw is almost an *Ashi-guruma* movement.

1984 World Championships: Karen Briggs of Great Britain scores with Tai-otoshi *on her way to winning her second under 48 kilos world title.*

Important Points

1. The lapel grip is particularly effective when placed under uke's armpit, because it is the lapel grip that has the task of pulling uke on to her toes.
2. The initial movement of bringing uke on to the throw is achieved by tori's left leg coming backwards in a half-circle. Tori's right leg should move across to block or trip almost as a reflex action from the left leg's half-circle.

Tip

Supple legs are extremely important in this throw, so all *Tai-otoshi* exponents should take particular care to warm up well. If the warm-up is neglected, a classic *Tai-otoshi* attack can end with a classic hamstring injury!

Wrong Leg Tai-otoshi

Introduction

This is not such a break from tradition as it may at first seem. *Tai-otoshi* is classed as a hand throw, and was originally taught without the use of the blocking or tripping leg. This unorthodox variation is really a return to that basic principle, using an element of surprise; and, although it looks both theoretically and practically suspect, it works. It is something that I saw happen in contest on a number of occasions and realised that it wasn't just an orthodox *Tai-otoshi* that had gone awry, but could be a technique in its own right. It is suitable for all users of *Tai-otoshi*.

Basic Technique

Uke anticipates a *Tai-otoshi* and therefore keeps the leg which is to be attacked far back. By doing this, she is actually making herself very vulnerable to her right front corner. Tori takes advantage of this by doing a half-circle

with her left leg (in a right-handed throw) and putting her right forearm under uke's left armpit. This, combined with a strong drawing action on the sleeve grip and the right leg blocking the opponent's near leg, has the unexpected effect of pinning uke on her feet so that she can be spun over.

Important Points

1. This works best when opposite grips are taken, for example, left against left.
2. Tori must use the lapel grip to slip past uke's defence. This is aided by a half-circle leg swing that must finish in quite a wide stance.
3. The real strength of the throw lies in the powerful rotation that is possible from this position.

Tip

This can also be used as an entry to the orthodox *Tai-otoshi*. It can unsettle or even make the opponent stumble and so create the opportunity for a full *Tai-otoshi* following a rapid foot movement.

Hikki-otoshi
(pulling drop throw)

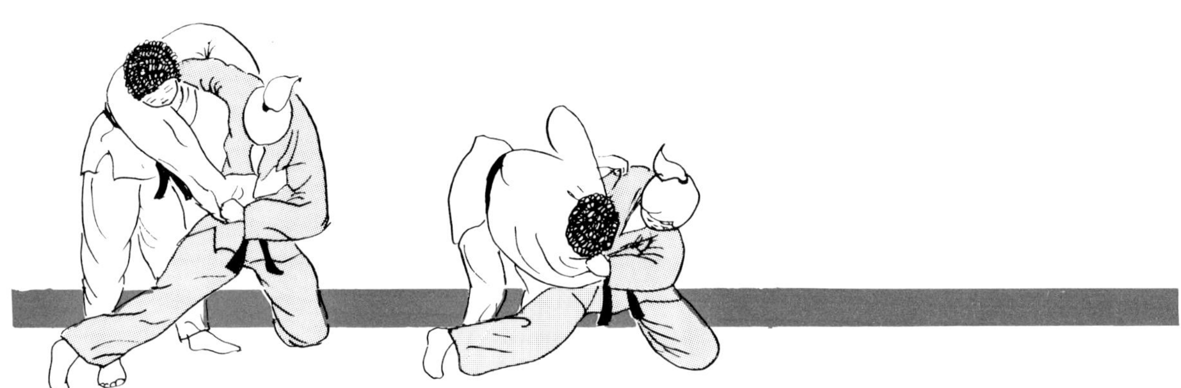

Introduction

The popularity of *Tai-otoshi* at all levels actually aids this technique, which is closely related to it. The two main ways of stopping *Tai-otoshi* are calmly to step over the outstretched leg, or to block with the knees firmly against the opponent's body. *Hikki-otoshi* is different in that tori is considerably lower on her left side (in a right-handed attack) than is expected, for she has dropped on to her left knee. In this sense, the sudden drop has a similar effect to *Drop Seoi-nage*.

Basic Technique

This throw is based on a fast pivot in mid-air, which turns tori, putting her into position on her left knee as her right leg stretches out to block. This is best done on the move; in a static position tori has no pulling power at all with her hands.

Important Points

1. Tori must drop and block at the same time – ideally, as uke is running on to the throw.
2. Tori's left leg can be placed outside, but in line with, uke's feet. This allows tori almost a scything action with the outstretched leg which can compensate for lack of hand power.
3. Tori's hands must be pulling uke forward at all times – only if uke is leaning over her feet is the throw possible.

Tip

Grips on the lapel and sleeve should be fairly low. If they are too high, the drop will mean that tori's own hands are stretched upwards, losing what little control they have.

OTHER DIRECT ATTACKS

Yoko-wakare Hopping Uchimata Makikomi
Kani-basami Morote-gari Tani-otoshi
Te-guruma

Yoko-wakare
(side separation)

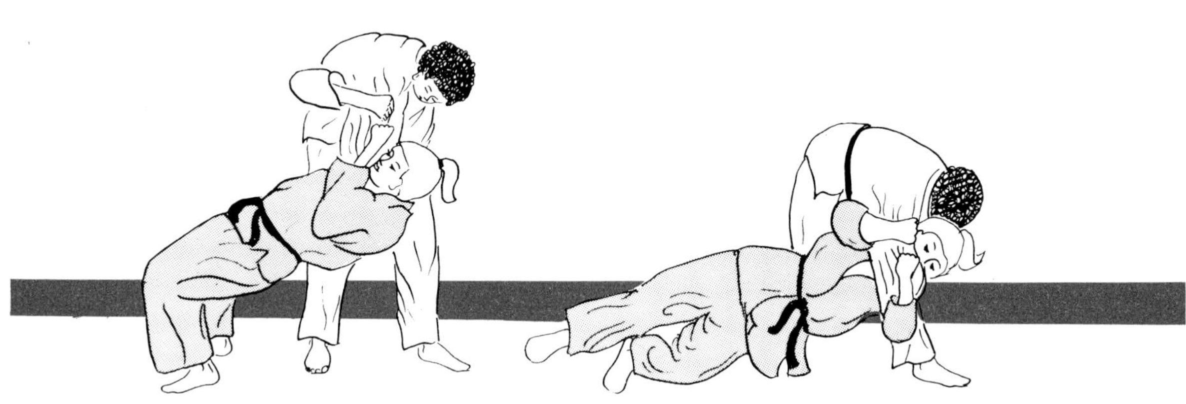

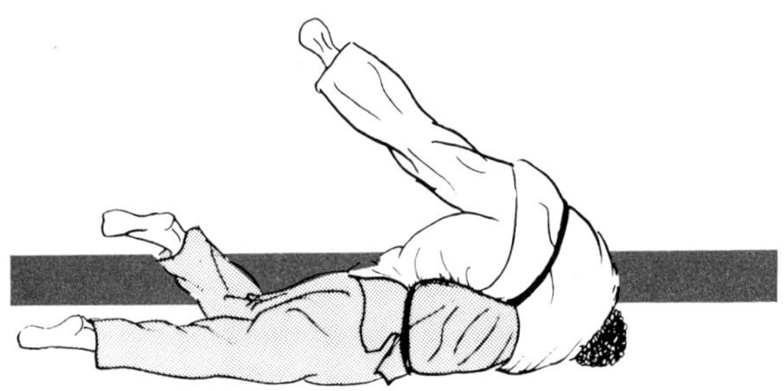

Introduction

This is only occasionally seen in competition or randori, but has proved to be effective, particularly against taller opponents. The opportunity occurs when the opponent has the dominating grip, pulling tori's head down, while at the same time having a bent posture herself. It can be used effectively by all weights.

Basic Technique

Tori turns inwards on to uke's dominating

arm and establishes a strong contact with uke's upper body. Having made the contact, she must begin to turn before she falls. The sudden shift of weight pulls uke off balance, but if tori's back is still facing the ground the danger is that tori will be taken straight down.

Important Points

1. There must be no contact with the legs at all – tori must step well across and out.
2. It must be emphasised that *Yoko-wakare* should only be attempted on an opponent who is bent over.

Tip

You can set the trap by letting your opponent bend you over.

Hopping Uchimata
(inner thigh throw)

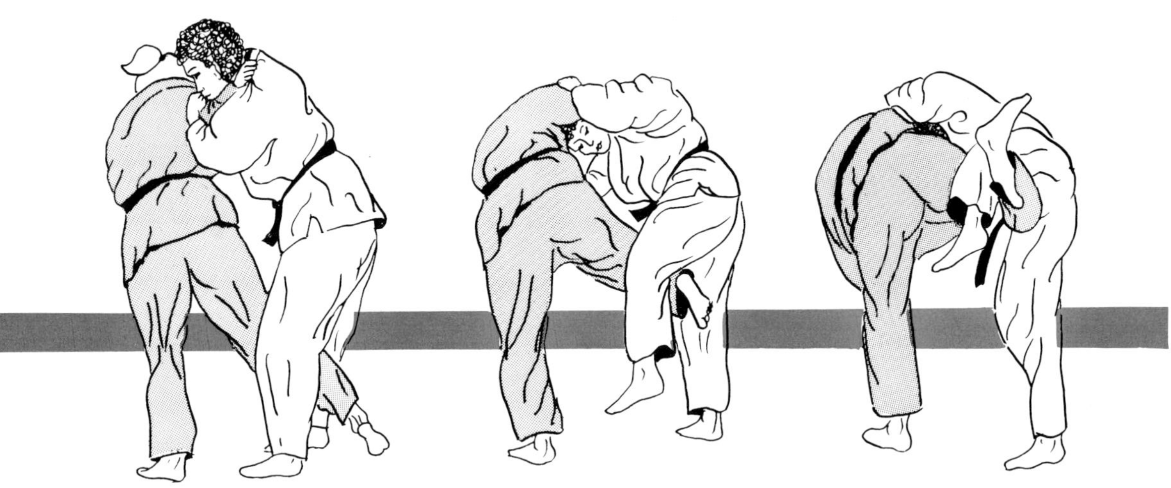

Introduction

A number of different *Uchimatas* are used in competition and in randori, but the *Power Uchimata* – where the attack is made straight up the middle of the opponent's body – is rarely used by women. Women instead substitute the power with rotation. Although this throw is used mainly by middleweights, it is increasingly entering all categories.

It is worth noting, however, that as training levels and strength factors among women increase, the power type of *Uchimata* is starting to emerge.

Basic Technique

The initial attack is against uke's left thigh (in a right-handed attack) in a movement which almost feels like an entry to *Ouchi-gari*. Uke lifts her leg to escape, but finds it hooked. Tori then hops round in a circle, forcing uke to hop with her. With each hop, uke's leg is forced higher until she can no longer remain upright on her standing leg, and a large throw results.

Important Points

1. This is best executed with a high collar grip. On all but very skilful players, a middle collar grip can have the effect of creating a barrier between tori and uke.
2. The collar grip serves to clamp uke's body to tori. If space is created, uke can escape.
3. Unlike most other *Uchimatas*, tori's standing leg should, with the first movement, be placed outside uke's left foot. This allows tori more room for rotation.
4. Once the entry is made, tori must use her sleeve grip to wrap uke's arm around her own waist and turn her head.

Tip

A useful training aid is to find a willing partner to hop round for as long as you can both endure. This allows tori to get used to the intricacies of control when circling on one foot.

1984 World Championships: Alexandra Schreiber of West Germany throws with Uchimata.

Makikomi
(winding throw)

Introduction

All weight classes should be aware of the basic principles of *Makikomi* because it is used, in one form or another, so frequently. However, it is mainly successful among middleweights and above because the rotating weight factor is such a central element.

Basic Technique

The *Makikomi* which is most successful for women uses a *Tai-otoshi* leg action. With a good sleeve grip as the base, tori moves her legs into a *Tai-otoshi* position while her free hand moves in a strong power curve over uke's upper arm. This action winds tori's body inside uke's outstretched arm and takes uke to the ground in a continuous rolling action.

Important Points

1. The strong power curve must be bold and uninterrupted if the throw is to be clean, and not a rather unpleasant drag-down, where collar bones are put in danger.
2. This power curve is helped by tori ensuring that she looks right round in a circle. If she just looks ahead and skimps on the visual circle, the impetus of the throw will be stopped.
3. It helps to think of the hip coming forcefully through in an *Ogoshi*-like action.

Tip

It is advisable that lengthy sessions of uchikomi are done on crash mats. This means that tori can attack without inhibition and learn to develop not only the correct technique but the complete commitment.

Kani-basami
(crab pinch throw)

Introduction

This is regarded as a dangerous throw throughout the judo world, and there has even been talk of banning it. The trouble is that, properly executed against an opponent who doesn't try to turn out of it when she is really caught, it is both effective and spectacular. It can be performed with a real flourish or more systematically and therefore can be used by all weights. Generally, however, it is the preserve of the middleweights, who seem to have just the right combination of speed, strength and weight. Its use should be considered mainly when the opponent has a marked sideways stance and tends to block forward throws with the hip.

Basic Technique

Tori's leg goes to the front as if to make an *Oguruma*, except that it is placed a little higher: at waist level or at least at the top of the thighs. Tori then pulls uke off balance sideways, and only when this is done correctly should the other leg be placed at the back of the knees. As tori drops in a sacrifice manner, she should ensure that the leg behind the knees is not stiff, but active. A high score can be obtained by using it to sweep high in the air, otherwise it is generally only a koka or yuko.

Important Points

1. Do not place the front leg lower than the thighs or the back leg lower than the knees. Injuries start to occur when both legs try to scissor at knee level.
2. The strong sideways pull is as important to the throw as the leg action. The pull and the directional control of the throw can be aided by having a grip on the back of the opponent's judogi at shoulder-blade level; but a lapel grip can also be used.
3. It is not advisable to jump in with both legs at the same time, because this makes accuracy of placement more difficult.
4. It is best to think of *Kani-basami* as a similar combination action to the *Uchimata-*

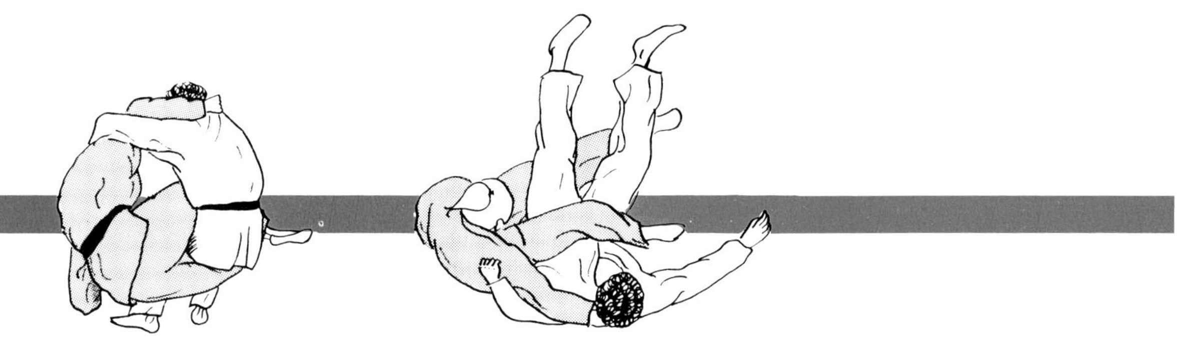

tani-otoshi Twitch, not least because its success depends upon uke resisting what she thinks is a forward throw by thrusting her hip forward.

5. Advice to ukes: if you see a *Kani-basami* coming, the best and safest defence is to bend forwards, not to try and twist out sideways and backwards as this is when injuries occur to the knees and ankles.

Tip

To train for correct placing of the legs, have a co-operative uke support you on the drop. After some uchikomi in this manner it is important to do the full movement, using the sideways pull to destabilise uke sideways.

Morote-gari
(double hand reap)

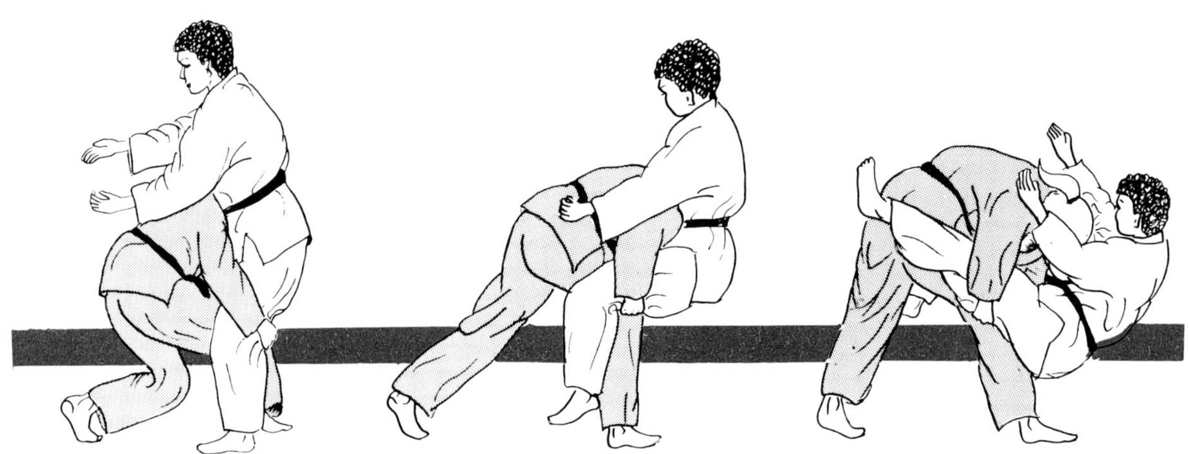

Introduction

Every judoka, male or female, tries this at some time in their careers, often when desperation is just starting to take hold at the beginning or end of a contest. Yet it is such a simple and direct attack that it works in all weight categories and at all levels. Even highly experienced players can be caught through a moment's lack of attention. However, few really study it.

Basic Technique

A feint to take grip is followed by a fencer's lunge. As the head turns to one side and the shoulder goes into the stomach, the arms reach out to grasp behind the thighs or knees.

Important points

1. Tori's feet must not get too close to uke; tori's body line must be similar to the position for a low *Ouchi-gari*.
2. The hands must not grip below the knees, as uke's weight will become heavier to lift.
3. The initial lift just takes the pressure of uke's weight off her feet. It is the drive from the fencer's lunge that does the rest: women generally lack the strength to lift their opponents straight up.

Tip

This throw is so easy to stop that tori must have the advantage of complete surprise. Either the attack is completely spontaneous or tori must be very skilful in disguising her intentions.

Tani-otoshi
(valley drop)

Introduction

This is a new Japanese variation of the standard technique, and is effective for all weight categories. Men's power can turn it into a spectacular *Uranage*-like action, but women tend to use it in a sharper, more skilful manner: the throw does not look so striking, but the fall for uke is equally hard.

Basic Technique

The opportunity for *Tani-otoshi* arises in a cross grip situation with left against right, particularly when a side stance has developed. In the illustration, tori is left-handed, while uke is right-handed. Holding uke's right sleeve with her left hand, tori winds her right elbow and hand over uke's outstretched arm, steps behind uke and takes her down. It feels a slightly unusual movement at the start, but can be effective.

Important Points

1. Tori needs uke to be firmly placed on the advanced foot, as uke can easily escape the technique by simply taking her foot out of tori's reach.
2. By setting up for the throw, there is the danger that tori will broadcast her intentions to uke. However, uke can be persuaded to put weight on the advanced foot by tori feinting a *Kouchi-gari* on the other foot.
3. Once tori is in position for the throw, the back of her head pushing hard against uke's body adds extra momentum to the throw. If tori does not control uke's body with the back of her head, uke can escape by coming round in front of tori (as has happened in the photograph).

1984 World Championships: Dawn Netherwood of Great Britain attacking with Tani-otoshi.

Tip

This throw developed because the sideways stance became more common. As standing armlocks are rarely seen in women's judo (probably because of the greater movement in women's joints) this becomes a useful technique against the standard stiff arm – although a sideways stance is essential.

Te-guruma
(hand wheel)

1980 British Championships: Jane Bridge winning the 1980 under 48 kilo British Open title.

Introduction

Te-guruma can be used both as a direct attack and as a counter (it is illustrated here as a direct attack). It is successfully used by women of all sizes, up to at least the 72 kilo category, because the lifting element requires more skill than strength. However, aspiring *Te-guruma* exponents must be able to move from a half-squat to an upright stance while holding a weight. The versatility of the technique makes this a particularly important throw to study as part of a basic repertoire.

Basic Technique

In the initial move, tori must get past the defending right arm of uke before she can decisively take up position. She does this by ducking her head under uke's outstretched arm. Once in position, tori must remain in the half-squat while clamping uke's body to her: only then can the lift begin. If tori straightens her legs too early she will be attempting to lift with her back; this is generally unsuccessful,

1986 European Championships: Karen Briggs of Great Britain.

because apart from straining the back it allows uke room to 'hook on' to prevent the throw.

Important Points

1. Tori must take a high collar grip with the right hand to ensure control of uke's head throughout this technique.
2. The role of the left hand is to clamp uke's body to tori and to assist with the lift. It is the right hand which, once uke is off the ground, does the main work of turning uke on to her back.

Tip

One of the best opportunities for the direct attack is when uke attempts to pull tori's head down either simply to gain a dominant position or as a prelude to an attack. Tori can resist momentarily, then suddenly duck under the arm and move in for *Te-guruma*.

The counter-thrower who uses *Te-guruma* often gives the game away by 'lurking' around, trailing the lifting hand and waiting for the initial attack of an *Uchimata* or *Seoi-nage*. It is better to practise by learning to jigotai and, automatically, searching for the *Te-guruma* opening.

COMBINATIONS

Ippon-seoi-nage into Osoto-gake   Ippon-seoi-nage into Kouchi-gake   Drop Ippon-seoi-nage with leg grab   Morote-seoi-nage into Morote-gari   Osoto-gake into Osoto-gari   The Twitch: Oguruma into Kosoto-gari

Ippon-seoi-nage into Osoto-gake
(one arm shoulder throw into major outer hook)

Introduction

Tori has to convince uke that the *Ippon-seoi-nage* is a real attempt, so that the swift change into the rear throw will come as a complete surprise. Because of the speed and change of direction required, this is generally a throw for the lighter weights, for whom it is a high scorer.

Basic Technique

Tori must know that the real throw is to be *Osoto-gake*. Tori turns in for *Ippon-seoi-nage*, but the back must not touch uke, nor must the right foot touch the ground. As soon as uke reacts by pulling backwards, tori's right leg snakes round, hooks and, with a half-circle hop, tori is in position for *Osoto-gake*.

Important Points

1. Tori's shoulder seems to rotate for the *Ippon-seoi-nage*, but actually all it does is allow the arm to clamp on to uke's arm.
2. As tori changes direction, uke's weight must be pinned on the leg that is being attacked.
3. The right leg is best thought of as a kind of floating *Harai*-type leg.
4. After hopping into position, tori's final movement before throwing is to use the chin to clamp on the arm.

Tip

Tori's head and eyes must be directed towards the ground behind uke, where she is to be thrown. If tori is not clear where to look, there is a danger that she will be countered.

Ippon-seoi-nage into Kouchi-gake

(one arm shoulder throw into minor inner hook)

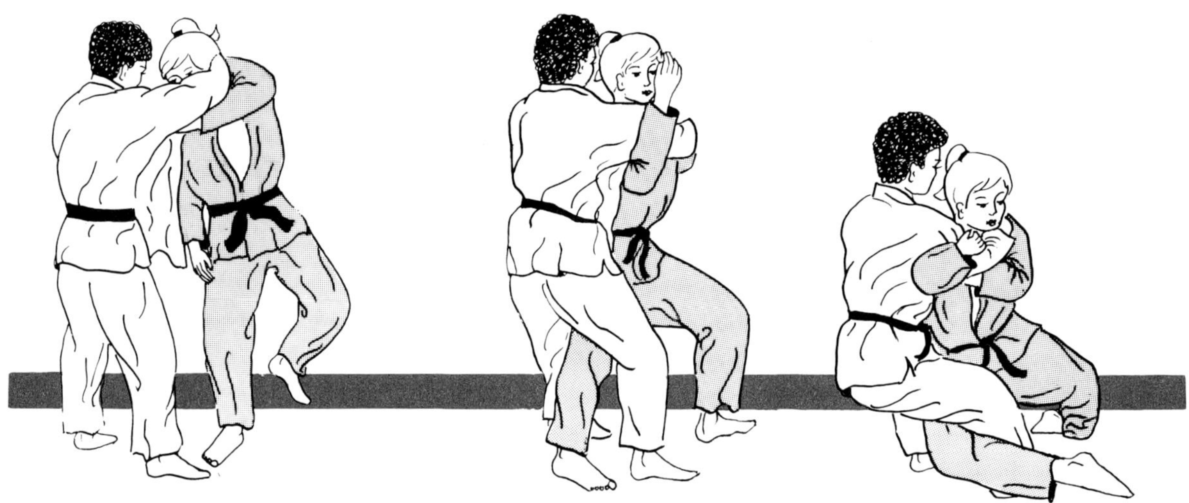

Introduction

This kind of fast movement attack is generally the preserve of the lighter weights, particularly as it calls for a half-circle turn in mid-technique. There is no reason, however, why balance control cannot be substituted for speed by larger women.

Basic Technique

The *Ippon-seoi-nage* must appear to uke to be a real threat, but tori must know that she is actually going for the *Kouchi-gake*, perhaps because uke has previously defended a *Seoi-nage* by bracing on her right leg.

Important Points

1. Tori's left hand must grip uke's right lapel over uke's right arm, as in the basic modern *Ippon-seoi-nage*. This allows tori to clamp down on uke's right forearm and gain a little extra control, which is as important in the *Kouchi-gake* as it is in the *Seoi-nage*.
2. Once into position for the *Kouchi-gake*, it is the back leg which provides the main impetus for the throw, driving the opponent backwards, rather than the hooking leg which just keeps uke in the correct position.

Tip

The *Kouchi-gake* works best as the sharp conclusion to a flurry of attacks against a defensive opponent.

1981 British Open Championships: Loretta Doyle of Great Britain and Edith Hrovat of Austria.

00 42
WAZA-ARI 1
YUKO 0
KOKA 0

Drop Ippon-seoi-nage with leg grab

Introduction

This is a small but effective variation on the basic throw, which can be brought into use if uke continues to escape by coming around the side even after tori has attempted to throw to the right. This is particularly useful against lighter weights.

Basic Technique

As tori throws, her right arm sweeps down to trap uke's right leg by the knee, pulling it in as tightly as possible.

Important Point

It helps to drive over uke's right leg, so that there is no chance of escape.

Tip

It is best to execute an orthodox *Drop Seoi* first and then add this variation when necessary. It is quite disconcerting because tori is suddenly attacking an unexpected part of the body – a general judo principle worth considering in a wider context.

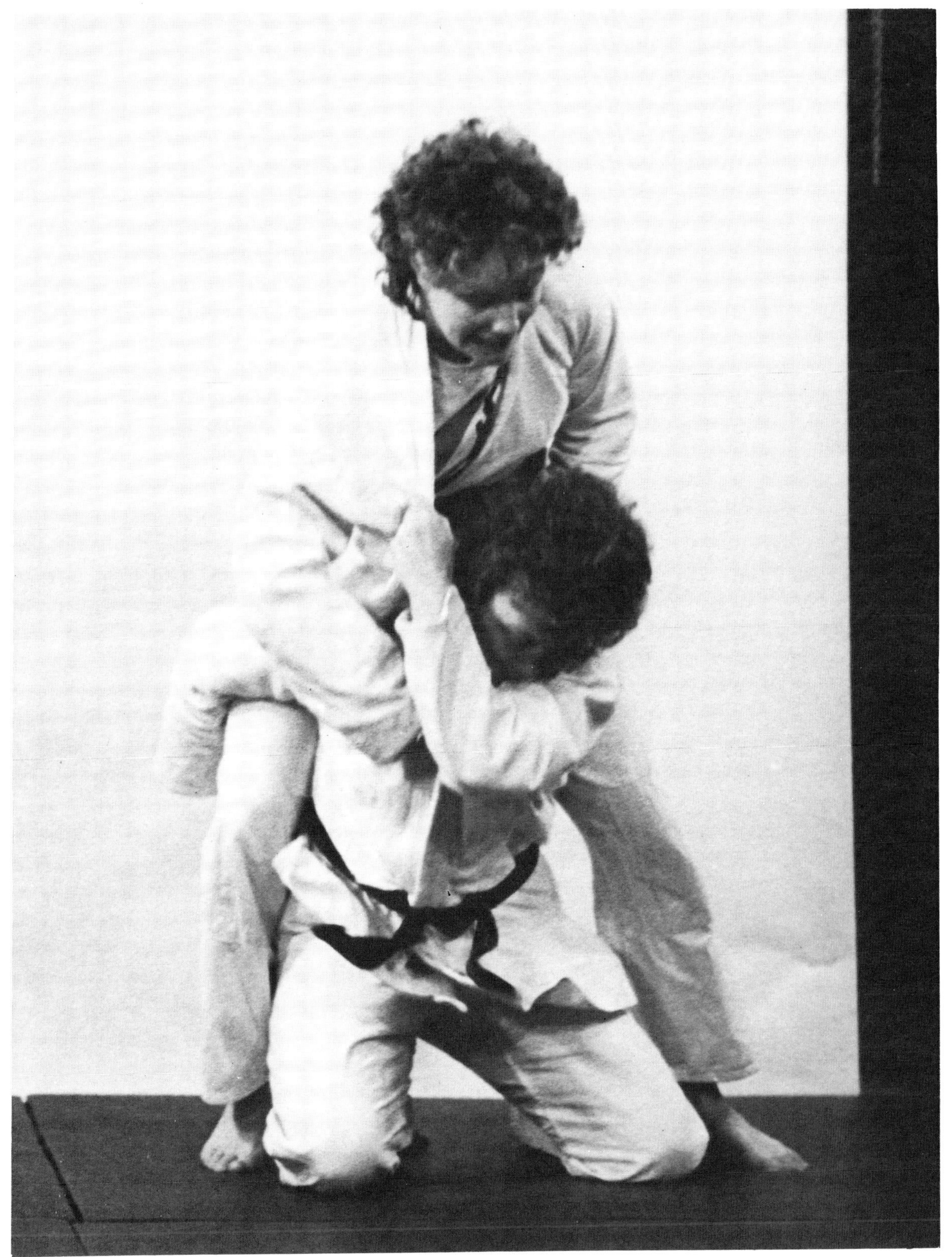

Morote-seoi-nage into Morote-gari
(double hand shoulder throw into double hand reap)

Introduction

This is a trick, which means that it will work once or maybe twice against an opponent. The surprise element is everything. It is very unlikely to work against someone who knows it is coming – although there are exceptions. It can be used by all weights.

Basic Technique

Having made some real attempts at *Morote-seoi-nage* or *Ippon-seoi-nage* only to find that uke resists strongly by pushing her hips forward, tori turns in fast for *Seoi-nage*, but without attempting to make any contact with the back. Instead, she releases her grips, rotates completely and picks up uke's legs at the back of the knees or the thighs.

Important Point

This works best in the repertoire of a *Seoi-nage* specialist, and uke needs to be 'set up' for it. The signal is an opponent whose weight is more on the back of her heels than her toes.

Osoto-gake into Osoto-gari
(major outer hook into major outer reap)

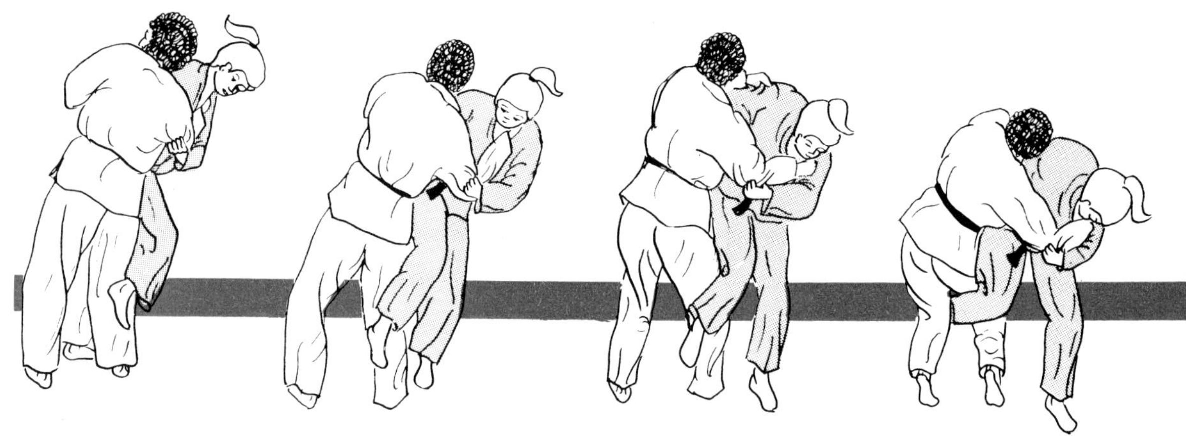

Introduction

The traditional *Osoto-gari* is rarely seen in women's judo because of the upper body power required to get into position for the throw – and yet, paradoxically, some marvellous *Osoto-garis* have been seen in women's international competitions. The reason for this is that the opportunity for an *Osoto-gari* usually arises from an initial attack involving a different throw. This is true of this combination, which can be used by all weights.

Basic Technique

Tori steps out and hooks behind uke's knee. If the gap between the bodies is maintained and the throw succeeds, it simply becomes *Osoto-gake*. The really big score, however, comes when, during the course of hopping around to effect the *Osoto-gake*, tori takes control of uke's head, forcing uke to try and step back on the hooked foot to maintain balance. This is when a strong reap from tori sends uke forcefully on to her back.

Important Point

The control of the head is the crucial factor. Two methods are relevant here: a middle lapel grip brought firmly against the ear, or a high collar grip with the forearm turned so that it comes forcefully against the back of the neck, bringing the head across.

Tip

This needs practice. It is not simply a question of making the most of an opportunity, for the reaping action must come just as the hooked leg stops being weight-bearing. If it comes too early the throw remains an *Osoto-gake* and probably results in a small score; if it comes too late uke will have escaped.

2

The Twitch: Oguruma into Kosoto-gari

(major wheel into minor outer reap)

Introduction

When well executed, this is one of the most spectacular and effective of all combinations. It is a classic action-reaction technique, which relies on a combination of perfect timing and perfect control. It works mainly on opponents who defend against forward throws with their hips rather than with their arms – their size is relatively unimportant.

Basic Technique

Tori must convince uke that a major forward throw is coming – a *Harai-goshi* or *Oguruma*. When the Twitch is being prepared, however, tori's attacking leg must at no time cross in front of uke. Tori just makes a twitch of the hips suggesting a forward throw, and uke's reaction is to thrust her hips forward in defence. As this happens, tori is already reaching behind with the foot to take either *Kosoto-gari*, *Nidan-kosoto-gari* or *Tani-otoshi* (as the final drawing shows).

Important Points

1. This only works against a good contest player. If you try it on a beginner in randori it may not work because the beginner simply doesn't know enough to be afraid of the *Oguruma* danger in the first place. In this case, you can probably throw to the front without too much difficulty.
2. Tori must be comfortable with an upright posture.
3. Double lapel grip can be very effective in addition to standard grip. Tori can pull down hard on both lapels and wait for uke to resist upwards. Tori then suggests the *Oguruma* and 'twitches' to *Kosoto-gari*. The attack is then a double combination.

Tip

Good hand control is required. The hands pull down and up and, once the opponent is launched, the hands must drive her down to the mat.

COUNTERS

Tsubami-gaeshi Kouchi-gari countered by
De-ashi-barai Uchimata countered by Tai-otoshi
Osoto-gaeshi

Tsubami-gaeshi
(swallow counter)

Introduction

This is a classic counter with all the advantages of simplicity and is of use to all sizes. It can be executed on the move or from a static position.

Basic Technique

As uke makes her *De-ashi-barai* attack, tori simply withdraws the foot from the attack. The foot then returns at speed to sweep the attacker.

Important Points

1. When attacked, tori does not take away the whole leg, but just bends it at the knee which removes the foot in an economical movement.
2. Any grip can be used for this counter, but continuous control of uke's upper body is necessary.
3. The countering foot must, as with all sweeps, be turned well in so that the sole makes contact. Ideally, the leg should be fairly straight and therefore strong.

Tip

It is possible to set a trap by leaving a leg forward and making it look as if it is a weight-bearing foot.

Kouchi-gari countered by De-ashi-barai

(minor inner reap into advancing foot sweep)

Introduction

This calls for extremely fast reactions, because the ground that needs to be covered at speed is considerable. It is worth practising, because *Kouchi-gari* is one of the most popular throws used by players both as a direct attack and to 'open' up opponents for big throws. The speed required for this counter makes it largely the preserve of middleweights and below.

Basic Technique

As uke attacks with *Kouchi-gari*, tori withdraws the threatened foot as quickly as possible. The weight must be transferred rapidly to allow tori's attacking leg to cross the space and catch uke's leg while it is still moving. The photograph shows how uke's stability is impaired by her right leg being overextended.

Important Point

This counter depends on a fast yet smooth response to the initial attack – tori's hands must control uke but her own movements must flow without any jerkiness.

Tip

The trap can be set by inviting a *Kouchi-gari*. This counter can be devastating when tori has some prior warning.

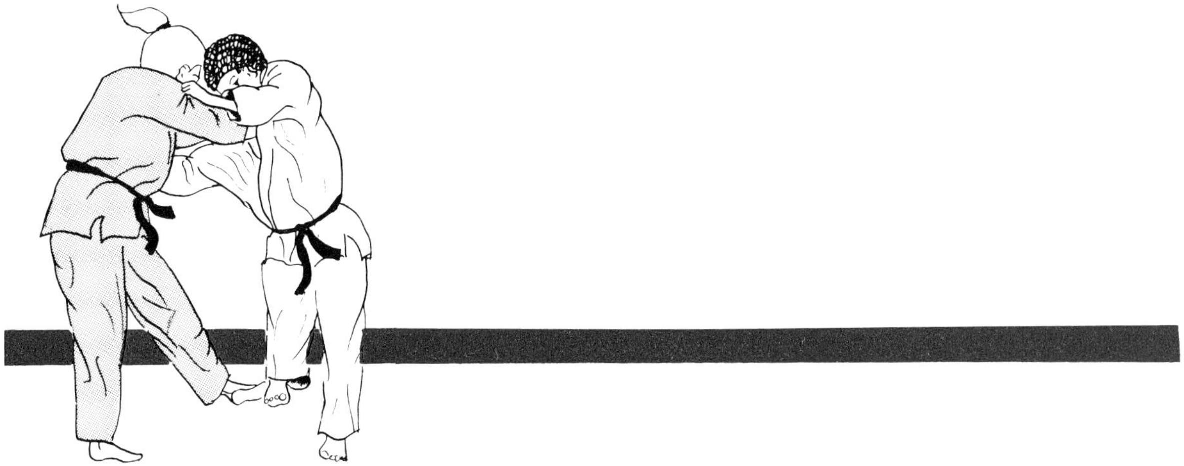

Uchimata countered by Tai-otoshi
(inner thigh throw countered by body drop)

Introduction

This is a crucial movement for women in judo. *Uchimata* grows in importance in women's judo as weight training develops, but in randori with men most women must find themselves attacked constantly with the technique. Even a brief study of *Uchimata* avoidance should therefore pay handsome dividends in daily practice.

Basic Technique

As the attacking leg of the *Uchimata* comes in, tori uses suppleness of the hips and speed to step in front of it, rather than attempting to ride over it. With the same motion, the active leg moves into a *Tai-otoshi* position.

Important Points

1. Tori needs to be aware that an *Uchimata* is coming.
2. It is important to keep loose and supple and to be confident that the attack can be avoided, rather than stiffening in defence.

Tip

It is relatively simple to train in this technique. It is beneficial both for the partner making the *Uchimata* attacks and for the avoidance practice. First develop a smooth avoidance action, and only then add the *Tai-otoshi* counter – which, incidentally, can often turn into a kind of *Ashi-guruma* action.

Osoto-gaeshi
(major outer reap counter)

Introduction

The use of *Osoto-gari* as a direct attack by women is rare and almost exclusive to the middleweight and above range; this is because of the fear of being countered and not having the upper body strength to stop it. However, out of a series of attacks an *Osoto-gake* can sometimes emerge, and this is where *Osoto-gaeshi* is useful.

Basic Technique

The opportunity for the counter arises because the initial *Osoto-gake* attack has been made without ensuring head control. Tori can then take the free leg in a half-circle and, with 'clamp' control of uke, turn and throw, almost in a *Harai-goshi* or *Osoto-gari* movement.

Important Point

For tori to have a realistic chance of success she must control uke's head, so a collar grip is crucial.

Tip

Once tori has started the throwing movement, she must look where she is throwing and fully commit the throwing action to that spot.

4 Newaza

HOLDS

ROLLS

STRANGLES AND CHOKES

Introduction

Newaza has always been the poor relation in judo. It is rarely as spectacular as tachiwaza – seeming to lack the speed, spontaneity and drama of a magnificent throw. Also, at the back of many people's minds, there is the thought that groundwork only ensues from the failure of a throw: in that sense, groundwork is really second best. There is also the traditional male attitude that it is undignified for women to grovel on the ground.

This view is both mistaken and immature. Tachiwaza may have all the sparkle and zest of youth, but in the hands of a newaza master groundwork reflects not only the quieter experience that comes with age, but an enduring understanding of the fundamental principles of judo. Many of the finest tachiwaza competitors have established their success on a base of natural talent, often relying on sheer instinct and physical aptitude. A newaza specialist, however, has often learned the hard way, finding that, although unable to build the necessary physical speed or fast reactions required by tachiwaza, she can raise her groundwork to a lethal level by the application of consistent, intelligent effort.

There are some young groundwork specialists, but generally the interest in newaza is for the mature judoka, who may initially have been prompted to switch interests because she felt she had reached her optimum standard in tachiwaza. She can learn new techniques, but to extend her judo she needs a change of emphasis, or at least a new area in which to work and improve. It is when the outstanding tachiwaza exponent establishes a sound and even inventive groundwork practice that a truly exceptional champion emerges.

In the many facets of women's judo, newaza is without doubt the most undeveloped area. This is strange for many reasons – not least because it is easier for women to practise fruitfully with men to develop groundwork skills than it is to develop throws. So perhaps it also reflects the preference of men for tachiwaza.

A commitment to groundwork has many benefits. There is no more certain way to improve competition results than to study groundwork. This is partly because the overall standard of newaza among women is not high. Yet the considerable number of opportunities for groundwork, aided by the frequency of dropping throws, means that anyone with skills in this area stands a much better chance of obtaining decisive scores.

In addition, it is clear that if you spend six months devoting as much time and energy to groundwork as to standing practice, your groundwork level will improve twice as much as your standing, if not more. Training in newaza is simply more reliable.

Finally, a woman who develops skilled groundwork suddenly finds herself showing more confidence in her standing work: her commitment to the throw is total and she is not so worried about a move failing and being taken to the ground. Her judo has a noticeably relaxed freedom.

Basic Technique

There are far fewer differences in groundwork skills in men's and women's judo, than there are in standing work, although the same problems of a general lack of upper body strength and a need to rely on movement exist. For instance, the basic hold down principles are the same, except that women need to be a little more cunning in their approaches and have to rely on feints and combinations on their turns into holds. In escapes, what they lack in explosive strength to create gaps is made up for by their extraordinary flexibility – women can escape by twists and contortions that make men gasp in amazement, although they do have to be a little careful of injury through over-extension.

The development of groundwork is an essential skills training, and uchikomi is as important here as it is in standing work. It is through the judicious use of uchikomi that an understanding of the basic groundwork attacking positions is developed – as time passes, a natural feeling for opportunities in more unorthodox positions will emerge.

In a sense, there are only two attitudes in groundwork: attack and defence. You can attack and defend from many positions, but the two most common in judo are when the defender is on her hands and knees while the attacker is on her back; or when one is on her back and the other is attempting to get past the legs. It is necessary to study the attacks and the defences from each of these positions. This can be done with male partners as easily as with women, so there should be no shortage of opportunities.

Every woman should have at least three basic turns in her repertoire for when her opponent is on all fours. She must be so familiar with those techniques that not only should she be able to turn most opponents of equal sex, weight and grade, but she should also have developed links between them – if the first one does not work, then by defending against it uke puts herself into a situation where she is vulnerable to the second or the third.

The regular uchikomi on these techniques should have a smooth fluency, both when done in sets of five or ten on each technique, or when done in sets of three, one after the other.

Similar movements involving set patterns should be developed for when tori is on her back with uke between her legs. It is possible to develop a range of turns from this position, although, for obvious reasons of gravity, it is more difficult. It is also necessary to study a series of techniques to get past the legs and into scoring positions.

Getting into position for those scoring techniques is one aspect of newaza, but it is important first of all to establish the technique for which you are ultimately aiming. Some women will have a natural predilection for holds, while others prefer armlocks or strangles. If at the start of a groundwork study the student appears to have no particular preference, it is a good idea to study holds, for these teach general control of an opponent, from which armlocks and strangles can develop. A sound understanding of hold downs should really be a basic requirement of a serious judo practice. In the end, there is no substitute for the primary practice of holding down partners and challenging them to escape. If they cannot, it is useful to try moving to other holds while maintaining control.

It is interesting to note that in competition holds are the most common groundwork scores, with armlocks coming second and strangles third. Women feel more secure with holds, and the skill necessary to apply armlocks is not as high as the skill required for strangles. However, because women's necks are not protected by so much muscle as men's, a study of strangles would probably bring good competition results.

Important Points

Women can learn much from groundwork practice with men, so long as their partners are sensible in the use of their superior weight and strength. At the very least, there is less chance of women being injured by a powerful yet clumsy attack. A relatively light woman could, for example, put a hold on a larger and stronger man and see how long she can control him. It is useful to ask the man's co-operation, suggesting that they begin by struggling fairly lightly and gradually increase in strength and urgency.

As in tachiwaza, the relative lack of strength means that women's newaza needs technical precision to work. Women should remember that they lack upper body explosive strength. Their groundwork should be based more on combining movement with the principle of using the arms to immobilise the opponent and the legs to turn. Western men rely extensively on their shoulder and arm strength, but Western women can learn from Japanese men in this respect – their use of legs, as another pair of hands, can be truly amazing.

It is essential to use the randori well. There is little point in assiduously developing nifty turns and secure holds if they are forgotten in the heat of the randori. A randori means free practice, and it should be exactly that: take risks, try the turns (on a systematic basis if you prefer), and if you get caught, search for escapes, try to create gaps, but then, if necessary, tap up and start again.

Perhaps the most important requirement for groundwork is a tenacious intelligence. If you study groundwork methodically but also with a lively mind, your standard of judo will improve dramatically – it is as simple as that.

Tip

A weight training programme is of particular benefit to a groundwork study. Judo practice can be a long and sometimes seemingly hopeless business, because the results take so long in coming and then often remain unnoticed until months later when a technique suddenly starts to work. Weight training, however, often shows an immediate effect on groundwork, so it can be a good idea to preface a groundwork study with a period spent weight training.

Even when women stop working the weights and begin to lose some of their increased strength, they seem to maintain most of their improved standard of groundwork. This may seem odd in theory, but it works in practice. Perhaps weight training gives women a confidence in their use of muscle, or perhaps women are not naturally as weak as they appear, but are simply unused to using their natural muscle power. This would explain why, in emergencies, women have been found to lift extremely heavy weights indeed. Weight training can have the effect not merely of building muscle bulk, but also teaching women what it feels like to pull and push mass – and that becomes a lesson which, in groundwork, they never forget.

Osaekomi

The follow-up from a throw is extremely important, for it is then that uke is at her most vulnerable. Once she has managed to take up position in a defensive ball, it will take a newaza specialist to break through the defences reliably – although this ability is also achieved through diligent practice. It is important, therefore, in training and randori to practise the follow-through and establish specific patterns of attack for dealing with the various angles that occur. Don't let uke settle.

In the best clubs, time is given for the practice of turn-overs, enabling women to develop their favourites. However, the practice of holding is often overlooked. It is necessary to spend some time practising holds, learning to pin even strong men with a combination of scientific application of strength and control, with a relaxed body. This does not come immediately, nor, in a way, can it be taught. It just comes from experience. When watching a top newaza expert holding even a strong opponent in competition, they seem to be expending very little energy, yet the hold is unbreakable.

Karen Briggs obtaining submission from Juji-gatame.

HOLDS

Kame-shiho-gatame　Kesa-gatame
Yoko-shiho-gatame　Tate-shiho-gatame

Kame-shiho-gatame
(upper four quarters hold)

Karen Briggs holding Veguillas of Spain with Kame-shiho-gatame.

Introduction

This is not a very popular hold with women, presumably because it relies so much on upper body strength from tori, enabling a supple uke to dislodge all but the best and strongest. However, it will increase in importance as women develop in strength; in fact, it already serves the heavier weight categories as it is more difficult for a heavy woman to get off her back once she is pinned.

Basic Technique

Kame-shiho usually works best for women from a throwing situation, so tori must be

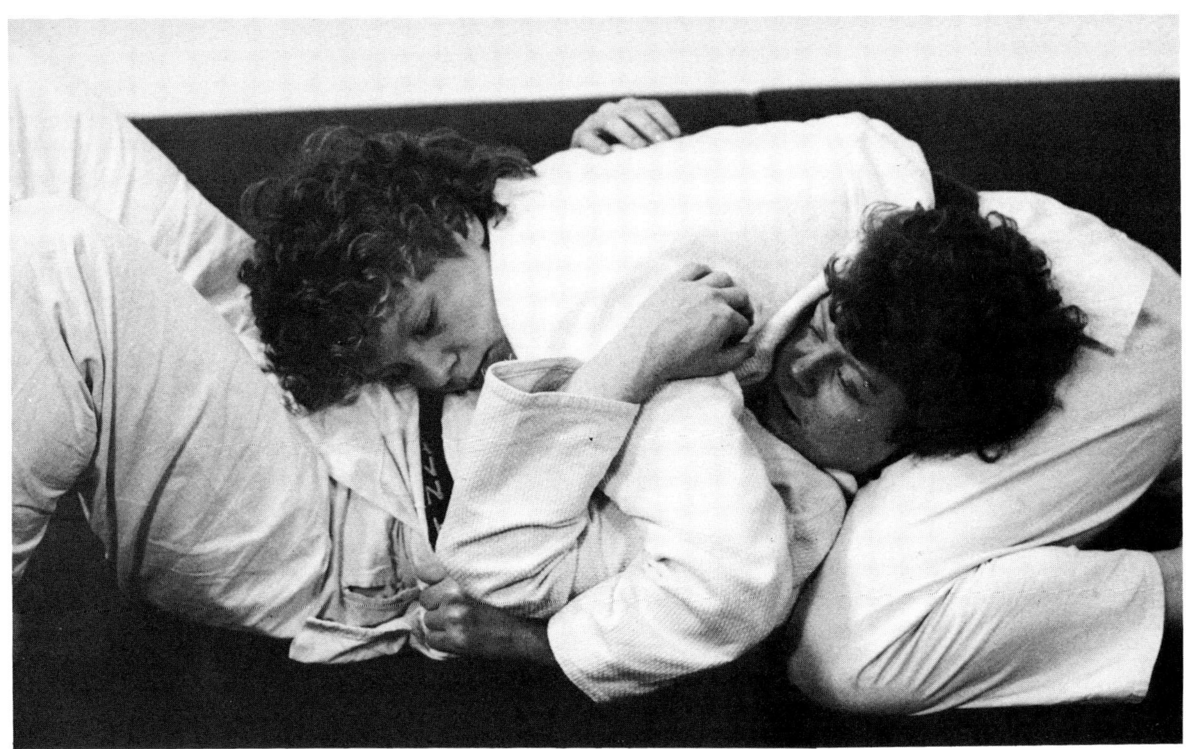

ready for the quick follow-through. This applies equally to *Kesa-gatame* and *Yoko-shiho-gatame*.

Important Points

1. The all-important head control can be achieved by bringing up the knees to trap the head. One useful trick is to place the head slightly on the thigh to immobilise it all the more securely.
2. In the classic *Kame-shiho*, where tori's chest attempts to control the head, uke often manages to work her head free, pushing it to one side. At this point, tori must control the head between her arm and her side to prevent any gaps appearing which would allow uke to escape.

Tip

It is worth practising *Kame-shiho*, concentrating on firm control with the arms, but with fairly relaxed and mobile legs, moving from a wide, even spread to more emphasis on one side or the other to combat uke's struggles.

Kesa-gatame
(scarf hold)

Introduction

This is usually the first hold to be taught to beginners. It remains the most popular one used by women, and is among the most successful in competition in all weight categories.

Basic Technique

The arm controlling the head should be slightly lifting the head in order to restrict the possibility for uke to bridge or twist out of the hold. The three other points of attention are

Avril Malley of Great Britain demonstrates good arm control under contest conditions.

the 'balance tripod' formed by tori's spread legs; the other arm firmly trapping uke's wrist and forearm; and tori's body weight pressing into uke's chest.

Important Point

For extra control, tori's head should be face down towards the mat.

Tip

In contest, tori often cannot achieve the classical control of uke's arm and may need simply to clamp it to her own chest, so practice for this form is essential.

Yoko-shiho-gatame
(side four quarters hold)

Introduction

Yoko-shiho would appear to be a hold dependent largely on upper body strength, but this is only partly true. It is gradually increasing in use among women as opportunities for it are more frequent than, for example, *Kame-shiho-gatame*.

Basic Technique

Yoko-shiho can be best studied by being aware of the three methods of escape. This enables tori to learn the principles of control correctly.

1. If uke attempts to sit up, tori has lost control of the head and chest. By forcing her own chest down (although the effort for the action often comes from the toes pushing off from the ground) tori can regain control.
2. If uke attempts to twist towards tori, tori must ensure she has adequate hold of the shoulders and neck, but the real control comes from the other hand by uke's legs. Tori's hand grasps the far trouser-leg and

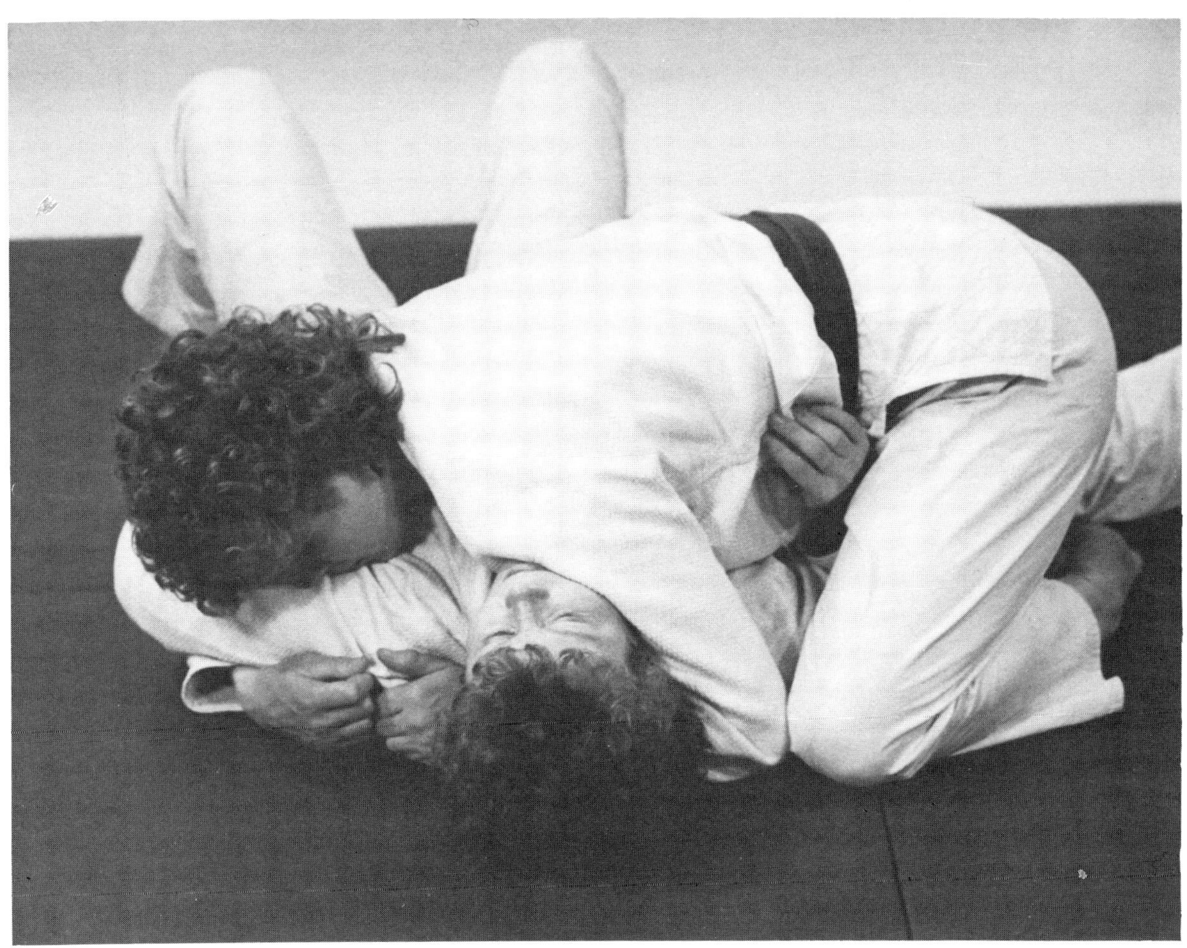

pushes away.
3. If uke twists away, tori should pull the leg towards her.

Important Point

As with all holds, it is control of the head that is the crucial element. Many women find it easier to change to a hold closer to *Mune-gatame* (as the photograph above shows).

Tip

If uke does manage to start rolling tori over her, tori can maintain grip but press her forehead on the mat to stop herself being rolled over.

Tate-shiho-gatamc
(four quarters hold)

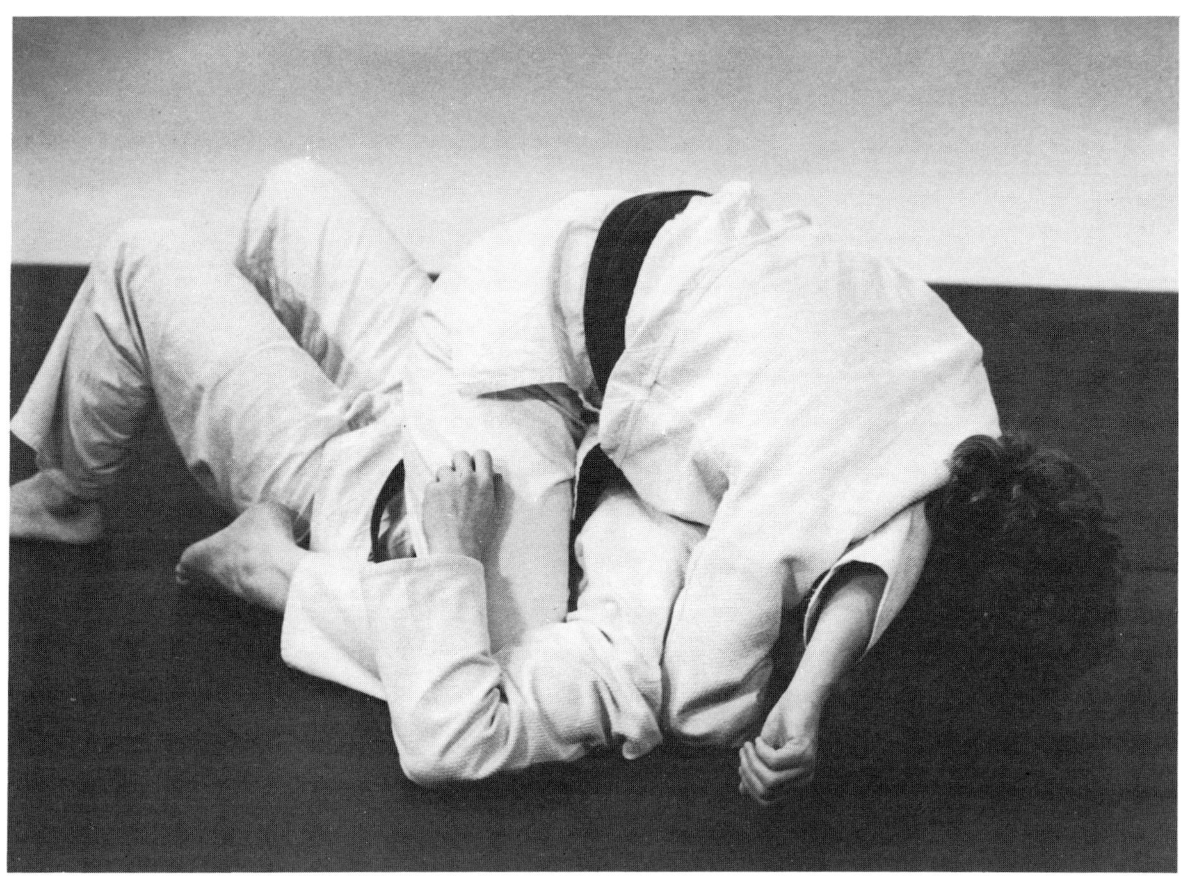

Introduction

This hold becomes increasingly important as women improve their range of turn-overs, for many turn-overs now used in competition, both from between the legs and when the opponent is on all fours, conclude in *Tate-shiho*. Really secure control takes time to master.

Basic Technique

Tate-shiho has a very wide range of variations, involving different placement of tori's body and arms. Like all holds, the most important single element is to control the head. One method of achieving this is to come extremely high up on uke's chest, but with the head and shoulders completely immobilised. If this is effectively done, the flexibility many women possess in the lower back and hips cannot be used effectively – they can only struggle to no purpose. Some women, however, prefer a lower *Tate-shiho*, with some weight from tori pressing on uke's midriff and the soles of tori's feet controlling uke's sides.

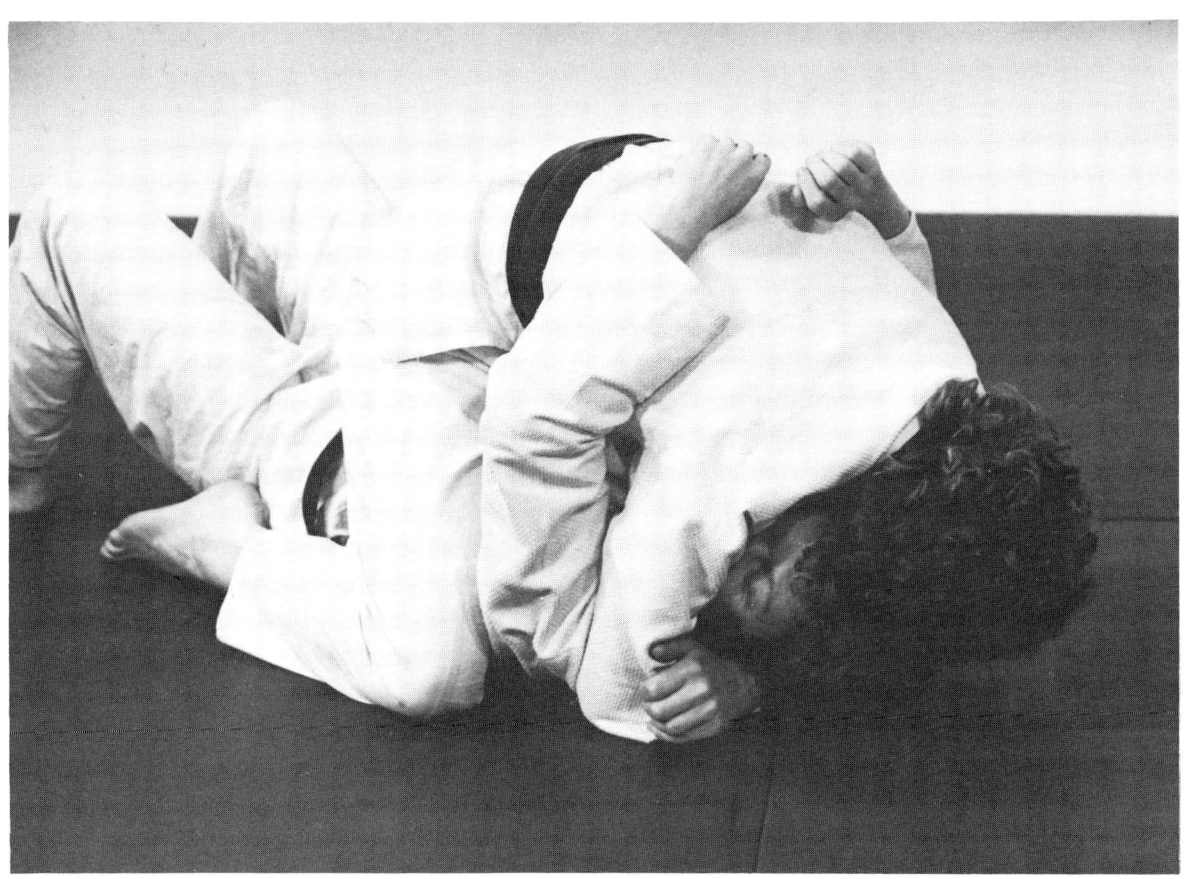

Important Points

1. It must be emphasised that head control is the crucial factor. It can be aided by tori clamping an arm with the head though this is rather difficult to achieve against an experienced opponent.
2. One arm can go down to take the belt under uke's body, but tori must still control the head with the arm pressing against the side of the head.

Tip

One great advantage of *Tate-shiho-gatame* is that if tori does lose control and is turned over, she ends up in a fairly safe defensive position on her back. In many of the other holds, a skilled uke can not only break out of the hold but in the same movement turn tori into a hold.

ROLLS

Double Lapel turn into Tate-shiho-gatame   Crotch turn into Osaekomi   Sangaku turn into Osaekomi   Roll into Juji-gatame   Leg and belt turn into Juji-gatame   Turn into Juji-gatame from underneath   Double Arm Roll

Double Lapel turn into Tate-shiho-gatame

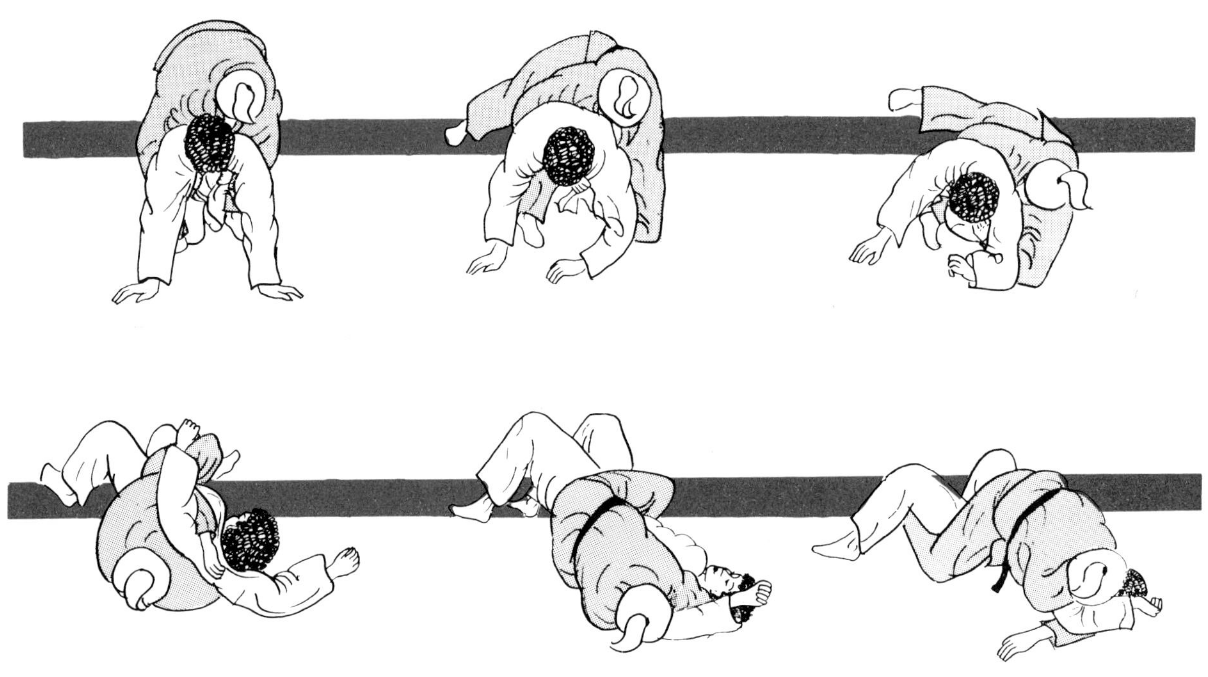

Introduction

This is a turn with the particular merit of using two lapel grips which can always be obtained, even from the most defensive opponent. The rolling action involved makes it relevant to all weight classes.

Basic Technique

Once the lapels have been grasped, tori pulls tight on both sides to prevent any loss of control at a later stage. Tori then clamps uke's body tightly to her own and rolls sideways. As uke tries to create a gap and escape, tori

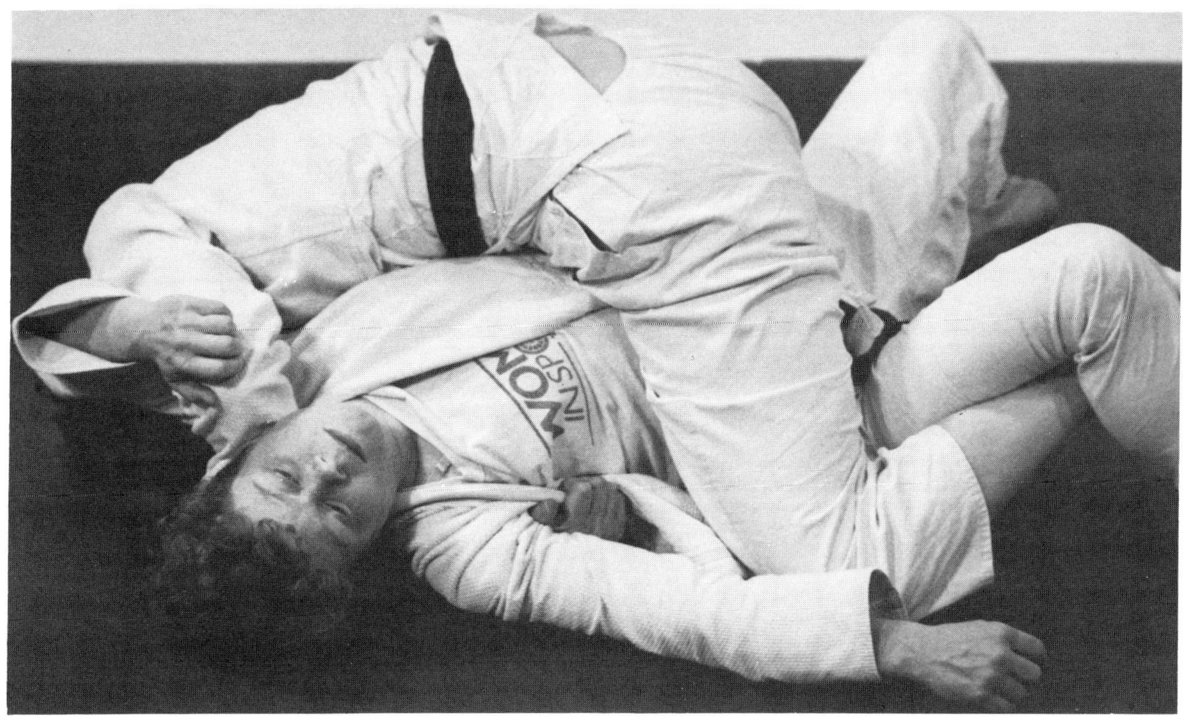

brings one arm under uke's arm and over her head, while maintaining a strong grip on the other lapel. The leg then comes over for *Tate-shiho-gatame*, with tori ensuring that the leg is not caught by uke.

Important Points

1. As in many groundwork turns, this technique depends not on speed but on control. Someone who has made a special study of this turn should be able to make it work even when uke has an idea that it is coming.
2. Control is achieved not only by using the arms to prevent gaps, but also by the deft use of legs.

Crotch turn into Osaekomi

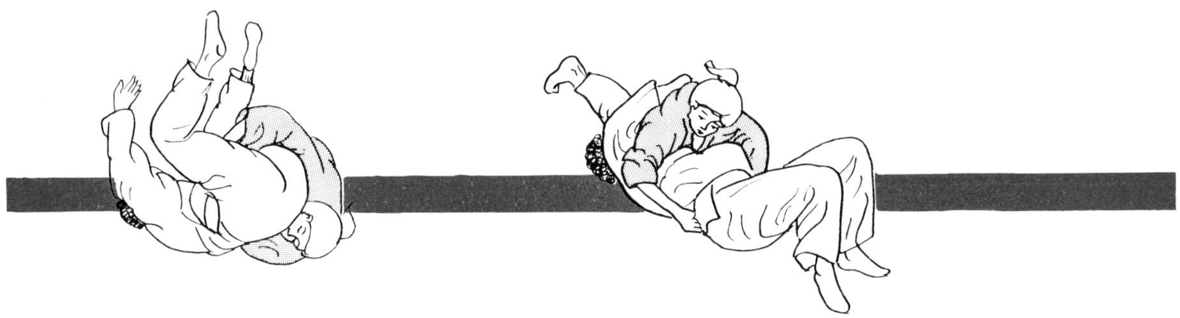

Introduction

This uses the same wrist entry as the *Sangaku* turn, but then changes to a completely different roll if uke blocks strongly. The stability in the all-fours defensive crouch depends on good balance on the two knees and two arms. This wrist attack takes away one corner, destabilising uke in that direction.

Basic Technique

With uke collapsed on one corner, tori grasps the crotch of uke's trousers and tips her over on to her back.

Important Points

1. A dynamic turn is needed, with full commitment of the body weight to tip uke over.
2. Immediately uke has rolled, the head and upper back must be collected with the free hand to control uke's head, otherwise she can gain her balance and turn away. Tori should end up in *Kuzure-kame-shiho-gatame*.

Tip

It is worth practising this in combination with the *Sangaku turn into Osaekomi*.

Sangaku turn into Osaekomi

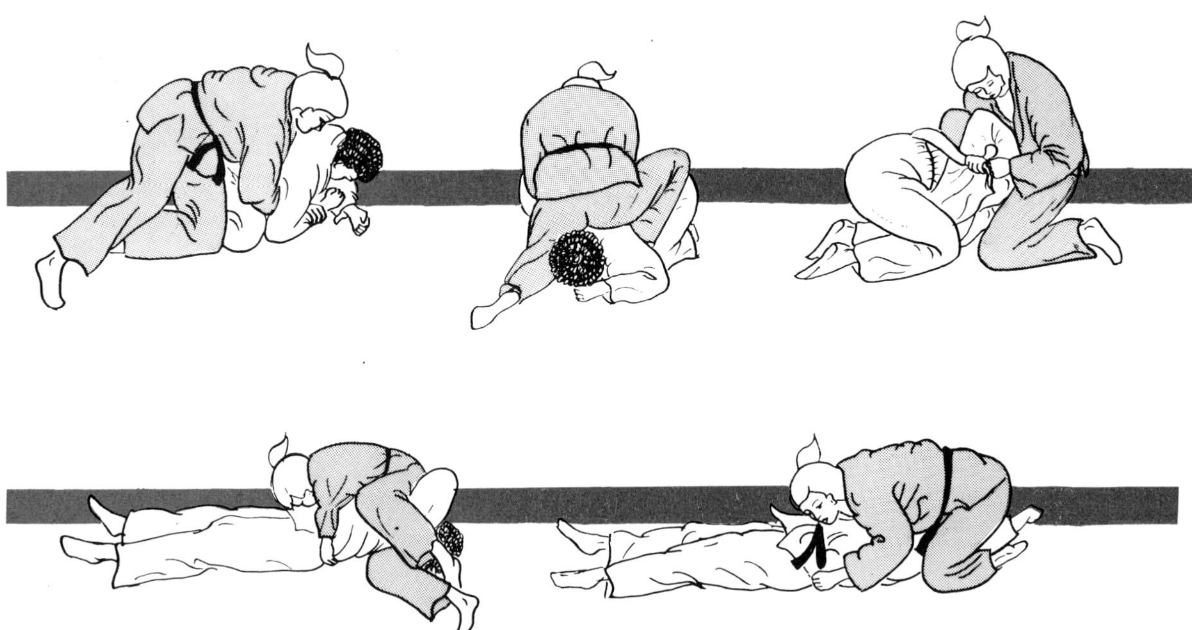

Introduction

Part of the reason for the effectiveness of this turn is that the initial attack suggests that a roll into the armlock is coming rather than a roll into *Sangaku-jime* or a hold. It is particularly useful against a tight all-fours defence.

Basic Technique

Tori's hand picks up uke's wrist. Only when she has good control does she move around the head, inserting her heel into the far armpit. The fall sideways puts her into the classic *Sangaku-jime* position and, while a strangle should be obtainable with women using the strength of their legs, it appears to be more comfortable for them to come up into the hold. Therefore, as soon as tori is on her side, she reaches out with her free hand to pick up the bottom of the opponent's jacket to tie up the arm. If the left arm picked up the wrist in the first instance, at this point it should be controlling uke's arm. The right hand then feeds the cloth into the left. Once the tie-up is complete, uke can uncross her legs and sit up into *Kame-shiho-gatame*.

Important Points

1. Tori should be crossing her legs, controlling uke, as she falls sideways.
2. The main way ukes tend to break free once tori is in the *Sangaku* position is by bridging backwards, thus preventing both the strangle coming on and making it very difficult for tori to sit up into *Kame-shiho-gatame*. However, tori can move into the hold by stretching out with her right hand and grasping the inside of uke's far knee. This helps to nullify uke's bridging attempts and gives tori a handle to help pull herself up.
3. It is also possible for tori to effect a hold simply by turning on to her face, with the help of a little leverage gained by grasping the outside of the other knee.

Karen Briggs half-way through the Sangaku *into* Osaekomi.

Tip

An unaware uke who leaves her top arm dangling in the air can present a chance for an opportunist armlock. Keeping the arm bent, tori can simply push the arm in the direction of her own legs.

Example of right hand feeding the cloth into the left to tie uke's arm.

Roll into Juji-gatame
(straight armlock)

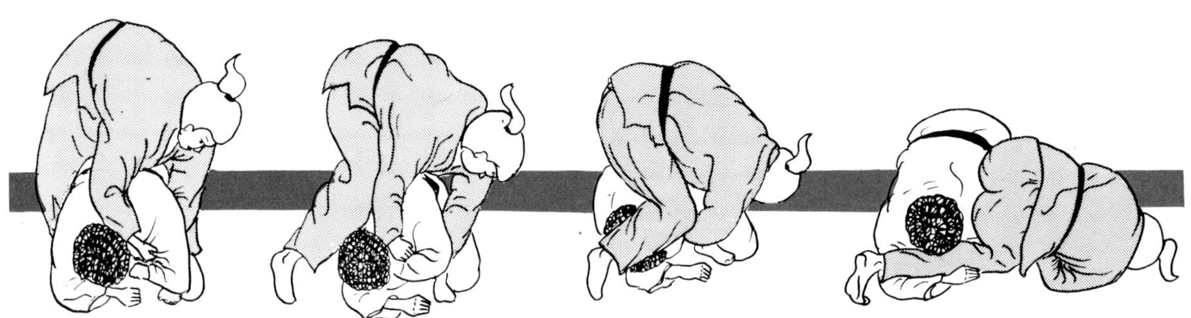

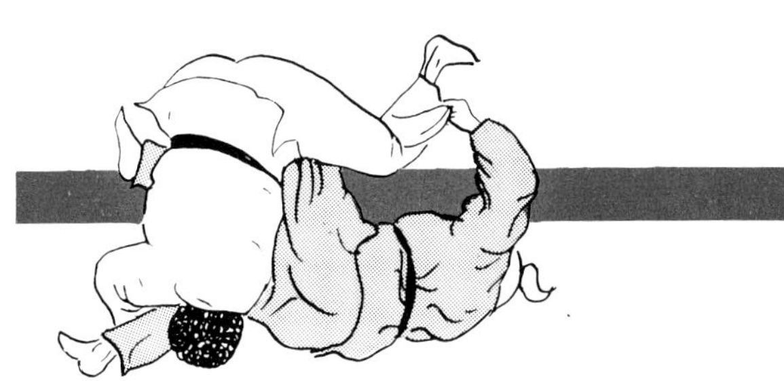

Introduction

This is one of the highest scoring techniques in women's competitive judo. The reason for this may not be that women are particularly susceptible to armlocks (their flexibility often makes the opposite true) but that coaches have been aware of the opportunities a defensive all-fours position gives to armlock attacks.

Basic Technique

Once on the back, tori takes one arm and hooks the leg on the same side inside uke. The other leg is placed with the shin on the back of uke's neck, giving tori good head control. Tori then turns away from uke (facing uke's feet) and, with the free hand, grasps uke's trousers and pulls her over into the classic *Juji-gatame* position. As uke falls on to her back, tori must rapidly bring her leg over uke's head so that both legs are controlling the body.

Important Points

1. Control, not speed, is important here. This move can be the basis of a long groundwork manoeuvre with tori turning uke again and again, until uke can no longer find the energy or the gap to twist out of the armlock and is forced to submit.
2. Throughout the turn, pressure on the arm to be locked must be maintained and, in fact, should actually tighten during successive moves.

Tip

If tori finds it difficult to break through uke's defence and straighten the arm, it is possible to sit up into a kind of *Kuzure-kame-shiho-gatame* hold and snatch back at the armlock if uke breaks grip in an attempt to stop the hold. Alternatively, various options exist for arm tie-ups to move into holds or *Sangaku-jime*.

Leg and belt turn into Juji-gatame

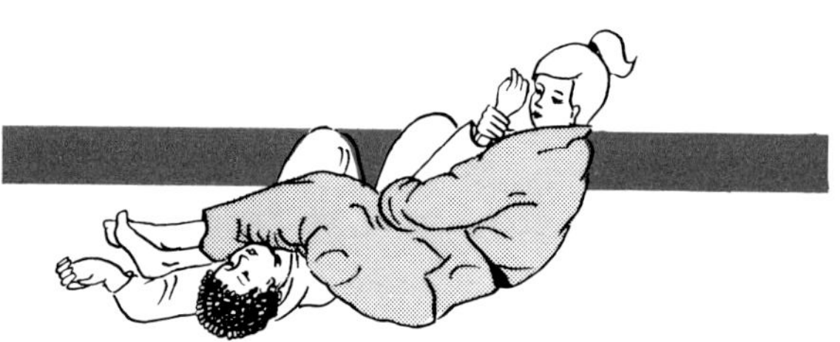

Introduction

This is a useful turn; it relies on the combined action of two hands and one foot to effect the roll, so precision of technique is more important than strength. There is a strong surprise element, because uke does not expect an armlock when being rolled over her head in this manner: everything points to an *Osaekomi* attempt.

Basic Technique

Tori sits astride uke and places her right foot into uke's groin. Reaching behind her, she picks up the belt with her right hand, swivels round, picks up uke's right arm with her left hand, and rolls uke over. The lifting and rolling action comes equally from the right instep, right hand on belt, and left arm. As uke starts to flatten out, tori swiftly brings her foot over uke's head into the standard *Juji-gatame* position.

Important Point

On the roll, tori adds a flicking action with her instep to speed uke's descent.

Turn into Juji-gatame from underneath

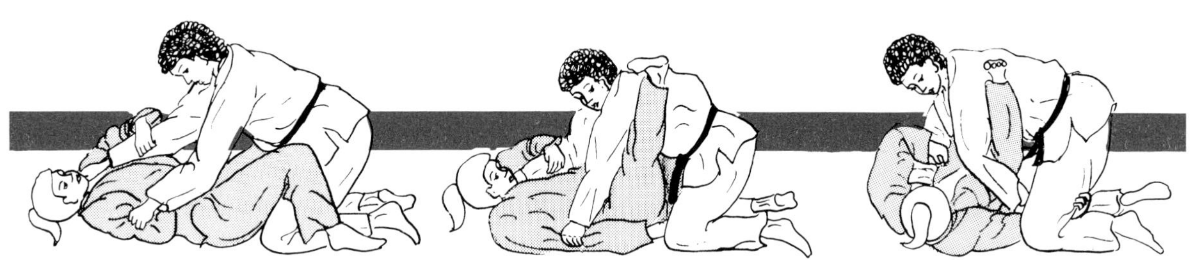

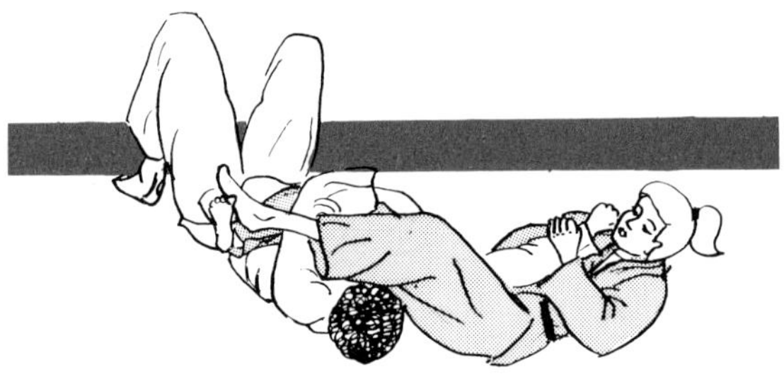

Introduction

This is another surprise technique because the attack is made from underneath, when tori is on her back with uke between her legs.

Basic Technique

First of all, space must be created between uke and tori; this turn cannot be done if they are chest to chest. Tori moves her head to the opposite side of the arm she is attacking – effectively, she is searching to adopt the standard *Juji-gatame* position, but upside down. If her head has turned to the right, she releases her right arm and grabs the inside of uke's left thigh as her own left leg comes up against uke's throat. At this point, tipping uke off balance, it can be a relatively simple action to sit up into *Juji-gatame*.

Important Point

At no point during the manoeuvre must tori relax control on the arm she is eventually to lock, but she must not grab at it, for uke will realise the danger and snatch it away.

Tip

The defence to this move is for uke to stand up. If she attempts to do this, tori can prevent it by twisting her body further through so that her head is between uke's legs. This completely unbalances uke, almost throwing her into the *Juji-gatame*.

Double Arm Roll

Introduction

This is particularly apt for women, because they lack the upper body and triceps strength needed to free their arms once they feel themselves trapped.

Basic Technique

This time it is tori who is on all fours, and uke is attacking from the head end. Tori can, in fact, often manoeuvre herself so that she establishes this position. Uke's arms enter for an attack; tori takes both arms above the elbows and clamps uke's body to her. She then rolls sideways, with a strong movement of the legs. Uke is turned on to her back, with tori in a strong reverse *Kami-shiho-gatame* position.

Important Point

The success of tori's hold depends upon the arms being well clamped and a good spread of the legs – strong, yet mobile.

Tip

It is the surprise element that enables this roll to work. Once the arms have been clamped and tori is about to turn, that surprise can be compounded if tori makes a slight feint in one direction and then changes suddenly to the other.

Karen Briggs attempting a strangle.

STRANGLES AND CHOKES

Koshi-jime Sode-jime Hadaka-jime Kata-juji-jime

Introduction

A few introductory words about these two aspects of groundwork are appropriate here. As has been mentioned earlier, women do not have such developed muscle layers guarding the neck as men. This makes them more susceptible to strangles, which cut the blood supply to the head, and chokes, which cut the air supply to the lungs. Men have to push the muscle away to get at the carotid artery, but women can generally make a more direct attack on the artery. Much the same applies to chokes which often not only have a suffocating effect, but can be painful too.

Important Points

It is important to distinguish between the two. The object is to aim clinically for one or the other and not just to crush the neck in a haphazard fashion and hope for a submission.

Although the main attention is on the neck and throat, the success of strangles and chokes is just as dependent upon the control of the rest of the body, achieved largely by the legs and by using gravity, pressing the opponent into the ground.

It is equally important to know which hand is doing the strangling and choking. Even if both hands are around the neck area, generally one hand is holding the cloth or body in position, while the other is doing the damage. It is crucial to distinguish which is which.

The strangles which are usually taught first, *Name-juji-jime* and *Gyaku-juji-jime*, rarely work in contest nowadays, but are important for the principles which they establish. *Sangaku-jime* should work, because women's legs are strong, but, for some reason, it has yet to have a top female exponent. It has been my experience that a strangle on the left carotid artery is more effective than on the right, which may have something to do with the fact that the heart is on the left. It is a small observation that may be of use.

Koshi-jime
(hip strangle)

Introduction

This works as a direct attack from the ground, but is best seen in its application as a follow-on attack from a *Drop Seoi-nage* that has failed.

Basic Technique

As uke drops, tori steps around the technique while maintaining hold on the lapel grip. Often, at this point, uke's neck is left unguarded, at least for a moment, which is all that tori needs to gain control and, by pushing the hips through, put on the strangle.

Important Points

1. The wrist of the lapel grip must be in the right position to attack the carotid artery. However, a small adjustment of the thumb edge against the carotid is nearly always necessary.
2. It is the armpit that provides the powerful point of contact that puts the strangle on.

Tip

Uke must not be allowed to raise her head and escape. Tori must commit her weight to keep uke's upper body and head trapped.

Sode-jime
(sleeve strangle)

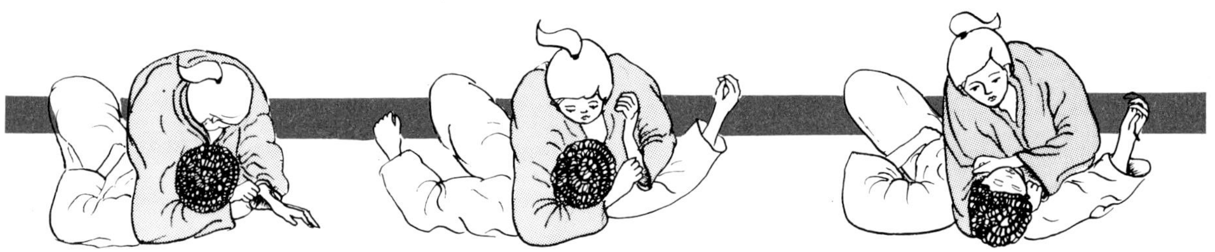

Introduction

This can be used when either underneath the opponent or on top of the opponent, though the latter is more effective because the forces of gravity can be brought into play.

Basic Technique

Tori is on top of uke, nearly in *Tate-shiho-gatame* but with one leg trapped. Tori puts one arm around uke's neck and deflects attention from the neck, perhaps by making an attempt to withdraw the leg. Tori then takes her sleeve half-way up the arm and puts on the strangle by pulling or twisting.

Important Points

1. If uke's head is turned away, the carotid artery can be attacked.
2. If the back of uke's head is on the mat, the choke is possible.

Tip

The surprise element can be central to this technique, so deflection of uke's attention is vital.

Hadaka-jime
(naked choke)

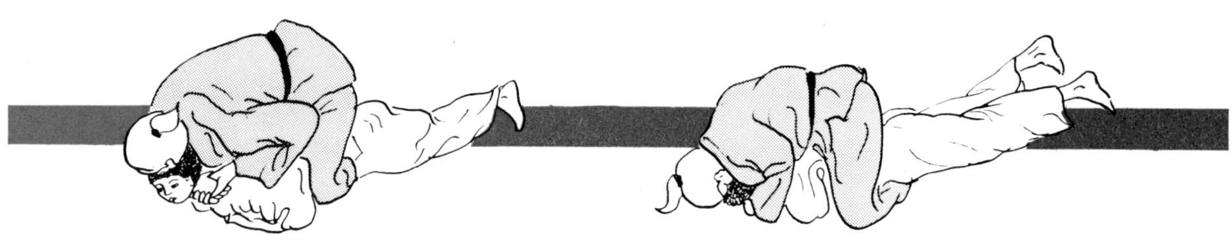

Note the hand positions.

Introduction

This has been effectively used at the top level since international competitions for women were first held, although it is very rarely seen in men's judo. Once again, neck muscle or the lack of it seems to be the reason. A specialist in *Hadaka-jime* must have considerable finger strength in order to find any gaps that exist in an opponent's defence. Tenacity is also needed, for *Hadaka-jime* rarely comes easily. More often than not, the opponent is simply worn down by constant attacks on both sides and from all angles.

Basic Technique

The base for *Hadaka-jime* is laid by good leg control. Tori leaps on uke's back and inserts her feet to flatten her. She then works for a good arch of uke's back – remaining aware of the spinelock rules. When uke's back is arched, her head comes up, offering the perfect opportunity for *Hadaka-jime*. Once the hands are in position, tori can apply the choke, but again must not put on a spinelock by pulling uke backwards without ensuring that her own chest is pushing down on uke's back.

Important Points

1. The key here is tenacity. *Hadaka-jime* is often used simply as a time-wasting manoeuvre, without realising the wearing effect that constant and meaningful attacks have on uke.
2. It can also be executed from underneath (as illustrated in the photograph opposite).

Tip

A characteristic of a potential *Hadaka-jime* specialist is long, strong tapered fingers – but with short nails!

Kata-juji-jime
(cross-strangle)

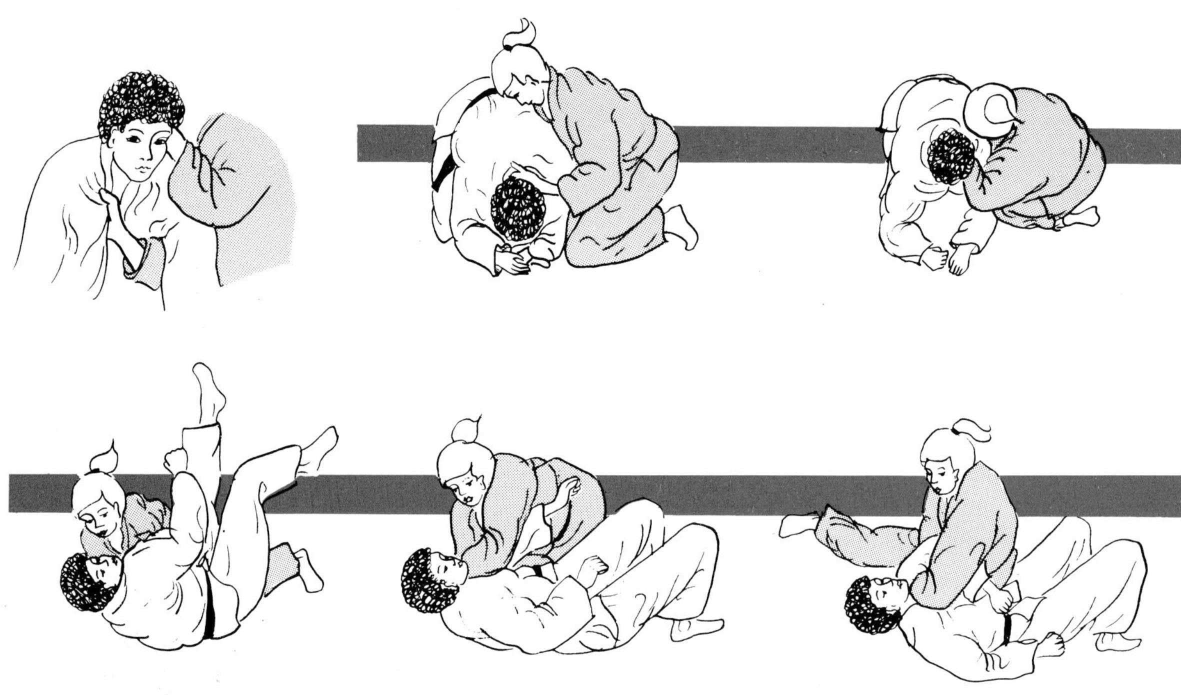

Introduction

This is a useful manoeuvre, because if the strangle fails there is an opportunity for a hold.

Basic Technique

The left hand enters position, taking a grip fairly high up on uke's lapel, but not so high as to suggest a strangle attempt is to be made. One of the strengths of this technique is its surprise factor – uke is expecting a turn-over, not the strangle that forces the roll. Tori's right thumb goes in under uke's collar at the back of the neck, and she then swings to the side in a vigorous movement, taking uke over her into a *Kesa-gatame* position. Usually, uke now submits to the strangle, but it is possible, if some hand control has been lost on the turn, to hold for the thirty seconds.

Important Point

The roll works because of the commitment by tori: a hesitant movement can end up with tori on her back and uke gaining advantage, although the positioning of the hands often prevents serious trouble.

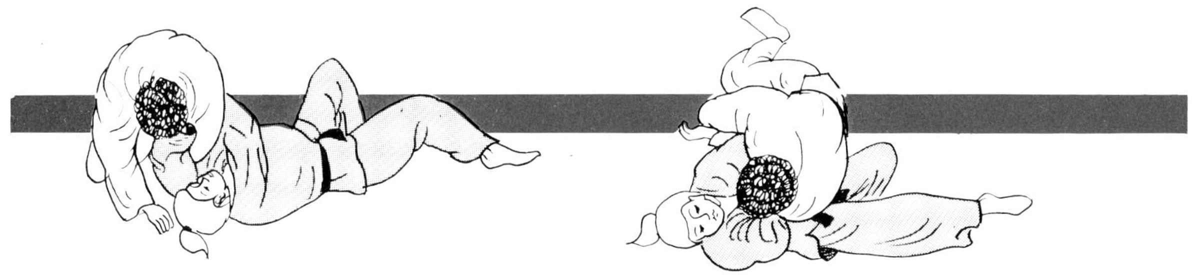

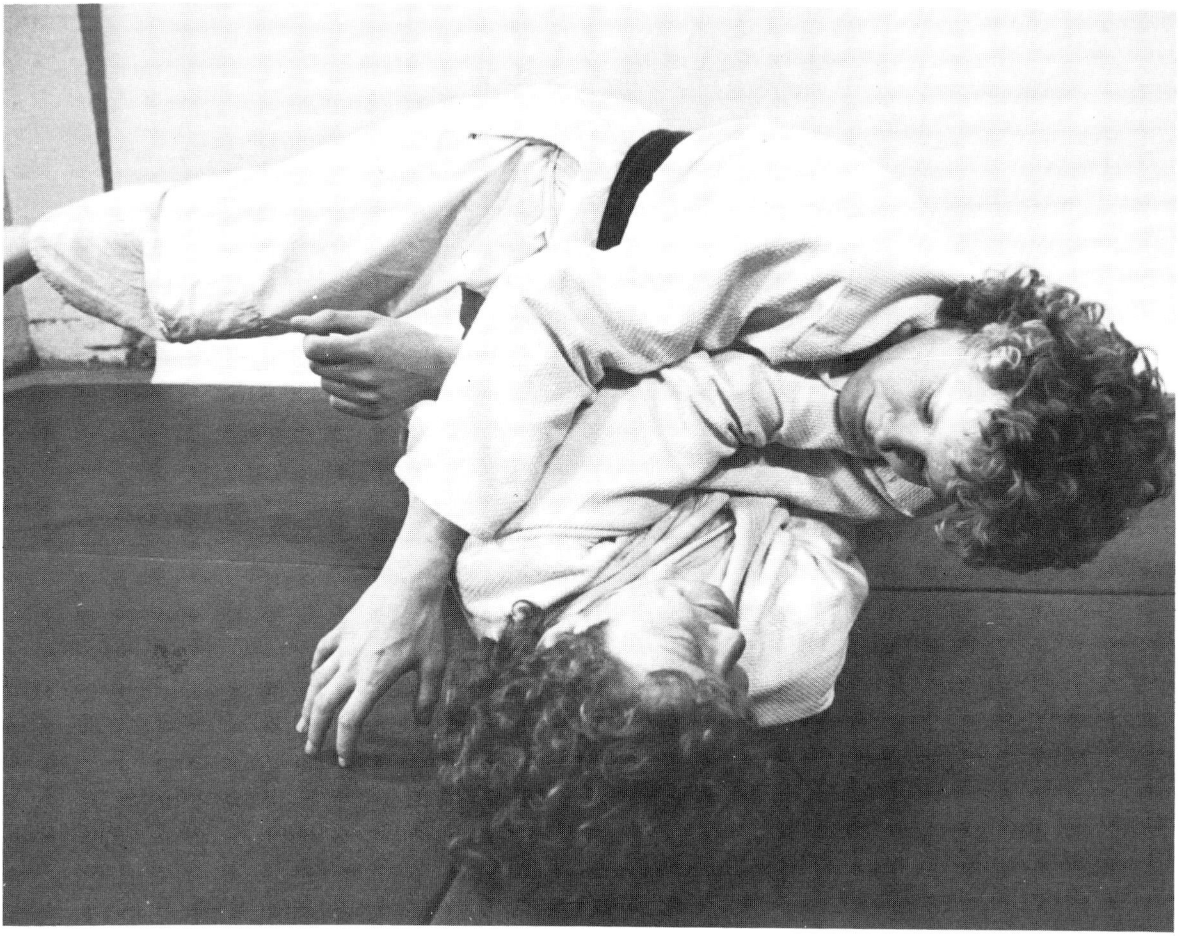

5 Training and Fitness

THE TRAINING OF JUDO SKILLS

There is a special satisfaction in the perfect execution of a technique in competition. Despite a strong defence from an opponent, a highly complex manoeuvre, performed at speed, results in a simple and definite conclusion – ippon! The feeling of the final thump of the opponent on the mat or the light tap of submission often remains in the body's memory for months. Even an experienced spectator can retain the image and 'feeling' of a particularly fine throw or groundwork move.

It is possible to admire the courageous or gritty qualities of a fighter who will not give up, who wears down the opposition simply by raw determination, but nothing in judo is so satisfying as a superbly demonstrated technique in competition – in other words, skill in action.

Definitions

It is important at this stage to distinguish between a certain technical understanding and the possession of a skill. A technique is an action that can be demonstrated with a willing partner. A skill is an action that works in competition or a strongly competitive randori, despite all the efforts of the opponent to prevent it.

This section is concerned with the means of developing firstly technical understanding and ultimately a skill.

Traditions

Since the foundation of judo, randori has been regarded as the best way of developing throws and groundwork moves to the level of a skill. Randori is free practice, and there are various kinds appropriate to particular circumstances – of which more will be said later. Free competitive practice is generally considered, both in Japan and most Western countries, as the most beneficial method. I believe that the acquisition of skill is generally based on 70 per cent randori and 30 per cent uchikomi, or repetitive practice, with a willing uke.

This applies, however, to a situation where there may be 200 Dan grades on the mat and the opportunities for a varied practice are unlimited. This may apply to men in most of the Western countries, but it certainly does not apply to women. There are simply not enough women to provide the varied practice that is needed from randori when developing a skill. Women either find themselves practising with the same few people again and again or, in a rather desperate search for variety, taking on men who tend to blunt the emerging skill rather than helping to hone it.

In these circumstances uchikomi increases in importance, and this is where much of the work in women's judo must be done. It has therefore been necessary to devise an alert uchikomi practice, rather than simply to go through the repetitive motions of turning in and turning out.

Training Partner

This highlights the importance of a training partner. Judo cannot be performed without a partner – or at least there is very little that you can do on your own – and a regular training partner, with whom a special bond is formed through hours of hard work, is an invaluable asset. In fact, it is very difficult to develop a skill without the active support and feedback that a good partner provides.

Your partner should ideally be around the same weight category, although not direct rivals, and preferably have about the same fitness level and aspirations. There are many exceptions to this rule: for instance, it is possible to follow the Japanese concept of sempai-kohai (senior student and junior student) although Westerners will probably prefer a less formal approach than is often seen in Japan. In addition, it is helpful when a friendship develops off the mat to complement the work done in judo. This becomes a practical realisation of Jigoro Kano's maxim of mutual welfare and benefit.

It must be recognised, however, that it takes time for a good training partnership to emerge. At the beginning the uchikomi is often a little rough, for the partners need to become accustomed to each other's movements. It also takes time to learn when to give feedback and when to remain silent. As time passes, both become aware of the other's technical needs. Even if they are studying different techniques, they develop an understanding of a wider range than they would by working simply with a succession of bodies.

Needless to say, those partners also share the responsibility for providing encouragement: to go out on training runs when feeling stiff and reluctant after a hard session the day before; and to push the weights with purpose rather than just going through the motions. What's more, they are there to lend support and give practical advice when a practice or a competition has not gone well, as well as being there to share the moments of success.

Coaches and Instructors

It is not impossible to develop techniques without a coach or an instructor, but it is more difficult. The experienced coach will see the long-term as well as the short-term implications, from the selection of a technique itself to an apparently minor detail of a foot movement. The coach will also be aware of the appropriateness of a choice of technique: whether it suits the body shape, the weight, the suppleness and the natural aptitude of the player concerned. The coach, however, must be able to demonstrate the technique to an acceptable standard; it is not enough simply to talk about it.

THE DEVELOPMENT OF A TECHNIQUE

Basic Uchikomi

The first stage in learning a new throw is always the static uchikomi. Straightforward repetition of the basic movement when standing still allows the player to look in detail at the whole complex manoeuvre. Some of the details that should be considered in this first stage are:

1. The basic body position and balance for the throw.
2. The function of the hands.
3. The function of the feet.
4. The head movement.
5. The direction the eyes should be looking at the point of throw.
6. The optimum position of uke's body at the point of throw.
7. The method or methods of entry.
8. The use of hands and feet in the entry.
9. Grip patterns.
10. The timing for the throw (i.e. when to throw).

This is just a short checklist worth considering

during the first sets of drills. It is also a checklist to which you may need to refer regularly throughout the development of a throw and even once it has been established in your repertoire. In the same way that a pilot takes his plane through a prescribed checklist as he warms up the machine for take-off, so the player should check over these points in each static uchikomi session before a practice. Minor adjustments are usually needed, and this kind of methodical care will pay enormous dividends in the ensuing practice.

Most practices start with static uchikomi and, unfortunately, the preparation tends to end there. This is, however, only the very first step in a training session and in the development of a throw. This is where tori learns the fundamental mechanics of the throw, where the first 'feel' of a throw begins to appear. As that develops, tori should start thinking of moving on to the next stage.

One-step or Two-step Uchikomi

Tori now requests uke to step in a particular manner, perhaps right foot forward and back. Tori begins to move in for the throw, using uke's movement. A smooth rhythm can be set, though this should not be too fast, for tori must remain aware of the checklist. What adjustments need to be made following uke's different body position? What is the best time to make the entry? What is the worst time?

The necessary adjustments can be identified by uke stepping in different directions and then adding a second step.

Tori then begins to direct uke in different one-step and two-step patterns with her hands, so that she becomes more like a puppet master rather than just reacting to uke's movement.

Grip Patterns

It is advisable to include some grip patterns at this stage, before moving on to larger movements. What is the best grip situation – conventional right-hand grips by both tori and uke, or opposition grips? Experiment with low sleeve and high collar, two lapels, and belt grips. Which grip by uke effectively stops the technique?

Power Uchikomi

A third player can hold on to uke's belt at the back, and it is now tori's task to try and throw both players. Working against resistance of this kind helps not only to develop power, but ensures that the mechanics of the throw are right. If they are not, the players won't budge.

Speed Uchikomi

Speed is an essential element of every throw, and at some point specific work must be done on speed entry. It is difficult to maintain awareness of too many points at once, particularly when doing speed work, so decide on one aspect which needs work and concentrate solely on that. In the speed uchikomi you are aiming to make the fastest possible turn – the effect should be a whirlwind, with everything around you becoming a blur.

Throwing Repetition

It is important to complete the technique, and this is where the crash mat comes in. Even with a sprung floor it is difficult for uke to sustain a long practice with high repetitions of hard and fast throws. It does not help if tori tries to throw gently: it hinders tori and hurts uke.

Use a crash mat well. At first, just execute the basic throw; then move on to one and two steps. Uke can begin to be a little obstructive with grips, to which tori must find the solution – and throw.

Tori can face six opponents, who are fed to her one at a time. She must grip and throw at speed, then get up and face the next one. This can be quite exhausting.

Uchikomi Problems

The first danger of uchikomi is that tori's mind becomes dulled by the repetition. It is important to keep a lively attention on what is being done; to achieve this high repetitions are not necessary, sets of ten or even sets of three may be sufficient. Skill levels drop when fatigue sets in, and the point of the exercise is to develop skill. It doesn't hurt, occasionally, to do something extravagant, like a session of 1,000 uchikomi on a throw. It is possible to learn about economy of movement, and how far you can operate fairly efficiently in a state of mental and physical exhaustion. However, the purpose must be clear.

A second danger is that uke does not give the right kind of helpful opposition. She must be neither a rag doll, nor a stiff body-builder. She must give a strong but realistic opposition, varying it according to tori's needs. Feedback is important here. If uke is unconsciously developing strong resistance, it can help just to throw in the opposition direction, 'straightening' uke out.

Bad habits will inevitably creep in – the checklist must be checked regularly.

Uchikomi on the Move

Once the basics of a movement have been established, it is crucial to develop the uchikomi on the move as the mechanics of the throw can drastically change. In this way, it is possible to achieve a situation fairly close to randori, without actually being strongly competitive. The static uchikomi will have begun to create some understanding of the technique and some muscle memory, which provide a basis for the next stage.

Movement Patterns

Women must rely more on movement than on strength, so this is where the major part of the work must be done.

Initially, tori must concentrate on specific movement patterns – making uke move on to the throw, and perhaps developing the half-circle leg swing to take up position. Uke can be made to step on to the throw by tori directing a movement pattern with the arms, or by stepping in a certain way, and eventually by combining – perhaps using a small foot technique to force uke to step as required.

These kind of movement patterns can be vigorous and dynamic, covering quite a wide area, or the movements can be fairly contained. Inventive action is the key.

Grips

Tori must learn to accommodate complex gripping within the movement patterns. Uke can vary her approach, sometimes being obstructive, then easing off, then being obstructive again, to coax sharper responses from tori, allowing tori to discover solutions to particular blocking movements.

Defences

Much the same applies to whole defences. As the practice develops and tori becomes accomplished in the technique, uke can begin blocking with her body as well as with her grips. Randori is now just around the corner.

Randori

Ideally, tori will not have attempted to use the new technique in randori until this stage. In practice, she will have tried it out probably from very early on, and even had some success because of the novelty, both for her and her opponent. However, months of only partial success will have followed.

Tori should now start putting the new technique into her repertoire of throws against much weaker opponents, those whom she could easily throw with her established techniques. As the months pass, she can expect to have some success with it against increasingly difficult opponents. It may take much longer – sometimes as much as a year – before it begins to work spontaneously in competition, and only occasionally it happens immediately.

Therefore, not too much should be expected from new techniques in a randori situation. It can be extremely satisfying when a new technique starts to work, and it is extremely frustrating when it fails, or doesn't start at all for seemingly ages. It is best to suspend judgement for some months, and to try to consider the results dispassionately, professionally.

A general word about randori for women: a serious player should have a very clear idea of the plan or purpose before a randori session begins. The flavour of the evening may be one particular throw – *Seoi-nage*, *Tai-otoshi* or *Tomoe-nage* – or a specific combination. It doesn't mean that only the new technique is performed, but that with each partner this is the main feature. It may be a session devoted to a methodical revision of the three or four main throws in the repertoire, or the new throw, counters, combinations or even defence movements may dominate. Only now and again is it worthwhile to go on without a plan, just to have a good fight.

The careful choice of partners is essential. In many dojos, older men enjoy practising with women and young girls as it gives them a rest from the tougher confrontations with competition-minded young men intent on sharpening their *Uchimatas*. Only a few, however, are able to give women a worthwhile practice, for they are too slow, too stiff and often too embarrassed to allow themselves to be thrown by women. On the other hand, women provide them with a good practice, for an 86 kilo man feels that in the end he will be able to power over a 56 kilo woman and feel grand. There is the added danger that if he cannot power her over he will become desperate, which is where the injuries begin. So don't be afraid to say, politely, 'No thank you' when approached by a man looking for an easy practice, although it is worth watching for the good men – experienced Dan grades, preferably lightweights, who will match movement with speed rather than strength.

Ideal randori partners for women are other women or blue and brown belt boys in their mid-teens. They have speed, technique and agility, yet while being strong they do not have a man's blocking strength. They also have a strong competitive spirit without an inflated ego to go with it. If in your club there are few women and few lightweights in the adult randori session, it does not hurt to search out the top junior class and use that for randori experience. This applies to women up to 66 kilos or so; the light-heavyweights and heavyweights can generally work fairly comfortably with men.

Fitness

The development of a new skill requires a certain level of fitness – it is as simple as that. If a player finds that she cannot do sufficient skill work because she has to keep having a rest, she needs to do some specific work on improving her cardio-vascular state and muscle endurance. It is worth remembering that once exhaustion sets in during a randori, survival, not skill work, becomes the order of the day. Even recreational players need to be aware of this and decide, very specifically, why they participate in judo – and is fitness they obtain through judo enough?

Feedback

In the end, a new skill is established by a combination of mental and physical study, and the development of muscle memory. With these factors, and the unpredictable element of time, the new technique should start to work in competition. It may take six months or a year for it to bed down sufficiently to work spontaneously at the moment of highest tension.

It does sometimes happen that there is no sign of it working, and the whole idea may need revising. This shouldn't happen if the work has been done under a good coach or instructor and with a good training partner. Throughout the period of learning there should be constant feedback between the three people, as well as other close training partners. However, even if a mistake has been made and it has proved to be the wrong throw for the individual, it will not be wasted time.

There is an old Japanese tradition which dictates that if someone wants to develop a little skill in judo, then the teacher takes the best natural qualities of the student and develops those. But if the student wants to develop an extremely high level of skill in judo, the teacher takes the worst qualities and works on those. After that, everything is easy.

Innovation

There comes a time with a new technique when the player surpasses the coach. The player has done so much intensive work on the technique that she not only plumbs its depths, but makes it part of herself. Instead of learning something by rote, she moulds it to suit her particular body movement or inclination. She discovers new aspects of the technique, perhaps in the basic action or in a combination. She becomes an innovator and adds to the growing encyclopaedia of judo itself. At this point, she is on a voyage of self-discovery: this is possibly the most exciting and ultimately satisfying area of judo.

Perhaps one day, she will throw a top opponent in competition for a superb ippon and the coach will come up to her and say: 'It was a beautiful ippon; a pity that the elbow was in the wrong place.' And the player will just smile.

Music and Judo

The amount of sheer repetitive work in developing judo skills can dull the mind. No matter how much the uchikomi practices or the cardio-vascular work are varied, they are, in the end, just drills that have to be repeated again and again.

This is where the stimulus of music can make all the difference. It may appear strange to the traditionalist to walk into a dojo and hear the insistent rhythms of pop pounding over the mats, but there is no denying the effect this can have on basic uchikomi, shuttle runs, circuit training and weight training.

I don't think music has a place in the dojo during randori, nor when skill work is going on and concentration on detailed work is necessary. Music then becomes just a distraction. Music can, though, relieve tedium and make even the boredom of shuttles or circuits palatable, and it can be used as a training aid. Anything from the latest chart material to Wagner – or whatever the players themselves want – can be used. Believe me, the work rate will improve.

A TWO-HOUR UCHIKOMI SKILL SESSION

The object of the following sample uchikomi session is to sharpen throwing and groundwork skills. This is a daily routine for top players, for it is a very intense session – or the kind of programme that would be run on a special weekend course for the national squad. It is constructed of uchikomi patterns that national calibre women would be expected to do most days in order to keep their established skill levels high. The benefits are as close to randori as is possible to achieve without actually doing randori.

For the example, four women of roughly the same weight and standard are involved.

Warm-up: 10–15 Minutes

This is a fairly comprehensive warm-up and suppling routine, covering the major muscle groups. The last five minutes or so would include some static uchikomi in pairs, to the left and right, backwards and forwards, and a variety of techniques. This uchikomi is part of the warm-up, using a range of movement. It is not regarded as a skill practice.

Static Uchikomi and Crash Mat Throws: 10 Minutes

The crash mats are now used. One woman (A) faces the other three. She takes B, does one uchikomi, turns out, turns in again and throws, hard, on the crash mat, contest style with no support. She repeats the pattern with C and then D. Then B, C and D take it in turns to perform the pattern, after which A starts again. Any throws can be used.

Even with four women this is quite a demanding practice.

Combination Uchikomi: 10 Minutes

A takes hold of B. She turns in fast for a throw, turns out and comes in for the same throw. B reacts as directed beforehand by A, and A throws on the crash mat with full commitment. A typical combination to use is the front-rear reaction *Ippon-seoi-nage* to *Osoto-gake*. A then repeats the pattern with C and D, and then B takes over the throwing spot. A variety of combinations must be covered during the ten minutes.

Counter Throw: 10 Minutes

B attacks at normal speed with a technique of her choice. She turns out, turns in again with the same technique at normal attacking speed, and A must counter. A can invite a technique, acting like a 'lurker' – such as leaving a foot out for *Kouchi-gari* which she counters with *De-ashi-barai* – or she can be completely spontaneous and just see what comes. A goes through all three opponents, then B becomes the thrower.

Half-circle Work: 10 Minutes

A asks B to run in a half-circle (180 degrees) towards a crash mat. A throws B on to the crash mat with full commitment. Any of the throws which require this kind of half-circle action are appropriate: *Seoi-nage*, *Oguruma*, *Tai-otoshi*, or *Makikomi*. The rotation is the central element of the practice. As soon as B has been thrown, A moves back into her starting position to take on C. The whole set should be briskly done, with no time wasted between partners.

Quarter-circle Work: 10 Minutes

The same pattern is repeated, but this time the half-circle run is cut down to a quarter circle, just 90 degrees. This sharpens reflexes and makes the players increasingly aware of changes necessitated by the different positions of uke. In contest, it is nice when an opponent obliges by stepping on to the throw, but often all that is given is a quarter-angle.

Rest: 10 Minutes

If the work has been well done, the girls will need a rest about now. If they want a small glass of liquid, that is fine.

Turn-overs 1: 10 Minutes

The women continue to work in a group of four. A throws B, who turns on her stomach as soon as she hits the floor. A moves swiftly into her turning routine. B makes her work for the roll, but doesn't block it completely. A then works with C, and so on. This is a good method of combining standing work and groundwork.

Turn-overs 2: 10 Minutes

This time A starts on her back with B between her legs. B is active, but is a partner not an opponent, and allows A, with difficulty, to effect the technique and roll over into a hold, an armlock or a strangle. A then works with C, and so on.

Hold Downs: 5 Minutes

Working in pairs, tori holds uke in one of the four basic holds: *Kesa-gatame*, *Kame-shiho-gatame*, *Tate-shiho-gatame*, or *Yoko-shiho-gatame*. Uke has 20 seconds in which to escape, after which they change round. All the four holds are practised, plus variations that each woman may use – for example, a special leg arrangement or grip.

Trapped Leg: 5 Minutes

Working in a foursome again, B lies on her back. A puts on a hold, but allows a leg to be trapped. It is her task to extricate the leg. A then works with C, and so on.

Direct Attacks on Crash Mat: 10 Minutes

Using the crash mat again, A throws the other three successively with stipulated direct attacks; perhaps only *Kouchi* and *Ouchi gakes* and *garis*. B then throws, and so on.

Attacks with One Hand: 10 Minutes

This is another throwing session, but this time with only one hand on the opponent: *Ippon-seoi-nage*, *Ouchi-gari* with the leg grab, a *Kouchi-gari* with leg grab, and so on.

The Box: 10 Minutes

Three crash mats are arranged on three sides of a square, and A stands a short distance from the open fourth side. She takes hold of B and they grip-fight their way into the box, where A throws. A then repeats the pattern with the others.

Finish

The women would now do their own warm-down, as they relax after what should have been quite a hard session. There are many other variations to these drills. Sometimes, instead of one or two of the drills, a 10 or 15 minute coaching session is introduced after the break in which new techniques or variations can be introduced. Alternatively, uchikomi can be done in pairs going up and down the mat, or instead of The Box the session can conclude with shuttle runs.

All this is specific preparation for randori and contest. The afternoon would be relatively free for resting before the evening randori, in which they would be expected to do quality randori, following a specific plan.

FITNESS

Fitness in judo is a relative concept. For many recreational players who perhaps do judo twice a week, it is a question of maintaining a modicum of fitness through judo itself. For competitors or aspiring national squad members, it is a question of getting fit and keeping fit for judo. There are many whose approach combines both attitudes, but it is a good idea to know which one is most important to you personally.

The intensity of a judo practice can vary considerably. It can be a fairly gentle business, more akin to kata than to combat, or it can be a highly demanding activity, perhaps one of the most demanding in the sporting spectrum – and for that level, fitness of the highest order is required.

Ideally, the best way of getting fit for judo is to do judo, but the hard nature of the activity, with its falls and confrontations inherent in a combat sport, means that such an approach is not practical. As fatigue sets in, co-ordination is lost and skill levels drop dramatically. This is where mistakes are made and injuries occur.

This is why supplementary training

becomes so important, and not just for the competitors. Many recreational players find the first randori enjoyable, but after that the session becomes increasingly arduous. Less attention can be paid to the acquisition and application of judo skills, as survival becomes the order of the day. In the end, judo is much more enjoyable and much more satisfying with a reasonable level of fitness.

The two main areas of fitness that need special attention are the cardio-vascular system (the breathing apparatus) and muscular endurance.

The Breathing Apparatus

The most efficient way of strengthening and deepening the breathing is running or jogging at a varied pace – a steady pace with sudden bursts of speed – this relates directly to judo. Long distances do not have to be covered – three miles is generally sufficient, but three miles on most days of the week for optimum fitness. As the leg muscles improve, the run will become appreciably easier and times will improve. There will soon be a noticeable improvement in fitness on the judo mat, as the greater breath reserves allow greater access to the skills. This applies not only to standing practice, but to groundwork as well.

However, it should be mentioned that even extremely fit competitors get out of breath. This is partly because there is a tendency to work to the maximum, and partly because while breathing is improved by supplementary training it can be dramatically upset by nerves.

It is surprising how much nerves can undermine the levels of fitness that have been attained. An attack of nerves – which can happen quite unexpectedly both in randori and competition – interferes with the breathing pattern. Normally, when an attempt to throw is made the breathing stops, but is resumed immediately afterwards. Nerves, however, seriously disrupt this ability to return to normal breathing. Each attack, even each movement by the opponent, tends to stop the breath and a severe oxygen deficiency is built up.

As soon as this starts to occur, it is important to make the most of each opportunity to breathe normally, for example a matte in competition. Even during periods of defensive inactivity, it is possible to regulate the breathing.

Shuttle runs are a great help in this area, for they constantly test the ability of the body to perform under the stress of oxygen debt and to breathe while strenuously active. The danger of the daily three-mile run is that you learn to breathe well only in a steady, rhythmic activity.

The main benefit of shuttle runs, however, is that they improve the recovery rates between periods of exhausting activity. A standard pattern for shuttle runs may be six sets of six 30-metre sprints with a partner, or perhaps in a group of two or three, with a couple of minutes' rest between each set. If the training is specifically geared towards judo competition, there is little point in training for more than the required four-minute length of each fight. You must bear in mind, however, that to reach a final you may have to win as many as six or seven fights, each of which could go to full time.

Muscular Endurance

A basic body circuit establishes the foundations for overall body strength and fitness. At a later stage it is possible to work on individual muscles for specific judo movements, but the base must be laid first.

Particular attention should be paid by women to upper body fitness and strength, for it is in this area that they can show the greatest improvement and make a major impact upon their judo skills.

A standard circuit of press-ups, sit-ups, squat jumps and squat thrusts serves most of the major muscle areas needed in judo. It is important to do each exercise well, not shirking on a full press-up, for instance. A small number of good press-ups at the beginning is better than a large number of jerks.

To give some idea of what top athletes are capable of in a simple body circuit and of the fitness levels in international women's judo, what follows are results from a fitness test given to members of the British women's national squad. The test was taken in the afternoon, after a morning of intense uchikomi skill training. The numbers vary according to weight, so the range has been given.

Press-ups: 2 minutes
Lightweight – 120
Middleweight – 75
Heavyweight – 55

Sit-ups: 2 minutes
Lightweight – 160
Middleweight – 110
Heavyweight – 69

Squat jumps: 2 minutes
Lightweight – 110
Middleweight – 71
Heavyweight – 47

Squat thrusts: 2 minutes
Lightweight – 170
Middleweight – 140
Heavyweight – 64

OTHER FITNESS CONSIDERATIONS

Suppling

A limited range of movement restricts the judo player, both on the ground and in throwing work. However, the judo player does not need the suppleness of a gymnast. For the recreational player, a general standard of suppleness is a bonus. The contest player, however, must have an additional and specific suppleness. For instance, there is little point in concentrating on hip throws if a player's hip movement is limited. If a leg stretch is minimal, concentration on *Uchimata*, *Seoi-otoshi*, or *Tai-otoshi* is not advisable.

Basic suppling should be part of each warm-up before judo and each warm-down after a session. The tendency to skimp on these by either omitting them entirely or just going through the motions results in a stiff body. It is as simple as that.

Gymnastics

A good range of gymnastic movements is certainly a bonus in judo. First and foremost, they help to develop spatial awareness – an awareness of where the body is in the air – which aids the avoidance of throws. It also improves general co-ordination. Head springs, hand springs, cartwheels, somersaults and some trampoline work are recommended.

Injuries

Injury is one of the occupational hazards of judo. It is important, however, to know which injuries can be safely strapped up and ignored and which injuries need time to heal.

Bruises, wrenched fingers or toes, black eyes, abrasions and cuts are not important. Cuts, however, do need local protection, because the sweaty environment of a judo session has a rich bacterial population. It also helps to tape wrenched fingers and toes, in order to give them a chance of healing.

Injuries to knees, collar bones, elbow joints, back and neck need more careful attention. It is possible to train around many injuries – a leg in plaster does not mean that the rest of the body has to go to waste – but advice from the doctor or osteopath and common sense are essential.

Diet

If you put rubbish in, you get rubbish out. A

judo training is among the most arduous in sport and a good body condition is required. Treat your body well – don't starve it, don't indulge it, and don't expect it to perform superbly on fast foods. Not even a Rolls-Royce will perform at its best on two-star petrol.

Overtraining

Lethargy, an inability to sleep at night despite being very tired, and a succession of minor and even major injuries, may indicate overtraining. When this is identified, the workload should be adjusted accordingly.

Rest

Rest and recreation is as important in judo as the hard work itself. The balance is crucial, not only for physical health, but for mental equilibrium as well. Without reasonable rest, anxiety, boredom or obsession set in. It is important to have a clear goal, and not to be deterred from that path, but a break from judo and training is necessary.

Ideally, that does not just mean flopping in front of a television. An additional interest is a very real benefit to judo itself, for it both refreshes the individual and, possibly, provides some unusual insights into judo itself.

Judo is one of the richest of sports in the areas it covers, but it can be very insular too. Complete insularity is not necessarily a good environment, especially for young girls.

Women and Fitness

There are no particular problems concerned with women and judo which are any different to other sports. Periods can cause fluid retention which makes weight control more difficult. This should be noted during competition times.

Intensive training can make periods irregular, as can the nervous tension triggered by competition, but this applies to all sports.

WEIGHT TRAINING

All sports recognise the benefits of a careful weight training programme, and women's judo is no exception. The equation, skill plus strength against skill, has a very simple answer. The increase in strength builds up a reserve that the judo player can call upon, which has an inevitable effect upon throwing and groundwork skills. The danger comes when weight training is substituted for judo skills, and a stiff defence or strong-arm tactics start to characterise a judo performance. This and the unscientific use of weights – just pushing heavy weights without a planned programme – has given weight training a bad name.

Women can benefit enormously from the use of weights. Few women are naturally strong, but through weight training they can increase their personal strength factor considerably. This means not only improving the effectiveness of their existing techniques, but making a wider range of techniques available to them. Weight training will enable certain throws, such as *Uchimata*, *Te-guruma* and *Osoto-gari*, to become a realistic possibility; only after special training will women possess the kind of upper body strength needed to execute these throws.

There is another benefit which is rarely mentioned. By increasing the muscle padding around the knees and shoulders, and by strengthening the arms, fingers and calves, the chance of injury is reduced. Women's bodies, initially so soft, become harder and thus more resistant to the knocks and strains that are part and parcel of judo.

The training must be balanced by careful suppling, otherwise a lot of flexibility can be lost. There is no doubt, however, that the end result is to the advantage of a female judo player.

Programmes

It must be said at the outset that weight

training is, in itself, a skilled activity, and on no account should individuals attempt to work out a programme for themselves without advice and supervision from a trained weights expert. What follows is more of a general guide, showing the way that weights can be used to benefit women judo players. A detailed training schedule must be worked out with a coach who is qualified to advise on weights.

It is generally inadvisable for girls in junior squads to do weight training; the later teens is early enough to start.

First of all, a foundation has to be laid. This can be done over a three-month period, divided into three phases.

Phase One The first phase uses very high repetitions with very low weights. This enables the body to become accustomed to working weights, as well as enabling the player to learn how to use them. Anyone who has worked weights over a period knows that it is not as simple as just lifting something and putting it down – skills are very definitely involved.

Phase Two The second phase concentrates on developing the strength factor. Here, the weights are worked in pyramid style, using increasingly heavy weights, but the emphasis is still on fairly high repetitions. This is where the main work is done on improving strength levels.

Phase Three The final phase is often the most painful – pushing very high weights with a low repetition factor. This work, against high resistance, hardens the enlarged muscles that have been stimulated by the first two phases.

Results

Most women find that this twelve-week course provides a thirty per cent improvement in strength levels. It can be a little uncomfortable and muscle stiffness will be experienced, but women will be suddenly aware of strength and muscle bulk and may feel that they are walking around a little like King Kong.

They may also feel somewhat slower in their movements, especially in their attacks, in the evening's judo. This may actually be the case, although often it is just a perceived difference. However, once this intensive weights' course is finished, a few short sessions on speed work will return the player to her normal speed. Attention must still be paid to suppling, however.

It must not be forgotten that when strength factors change, skills and movement also change. New skills will become available, but old skills will require adaptation. For example, a hopping *Uchimata* can become a power *Uchimata*, but the loss of a degree of flexibility in the arm could radically change a *Seoi-nage*.

Weekly Training

Once this foundation course has been completed, it is sufficient for most women to move on to a one day a week weight training practice, just to maintain the improved strength levels. The thirty per cent improvement in strength will gradually diminish over time, but about fifteen per cent can be maintained almost indefinitely with a once-a-week weight training session, lasting about ninety minutes.

Specialist Weight Training

It is possible to go further into a weights programme by devising particular exercises to benefit specific judo techniques. This needs experienced coaching, but is an area which is still developing.

Judo Benefits

The immediate effect of weight training on judo will be seen on the ground. The sudden input of greater strength often results in quite a sharp rise in judo newaza skills. Much of newaza involves working against resistance – not in the sense of brute strength just pushing someone away, but in the sense of creating a small gap for an escape or pulling an opponent close in order to control her.

The twelve-week course working with weights will also have cleared away any inhibitions women may have, because of their environmental training, in committing themselves in a muscular manner. For example, they become aware, perhaps for the first time, of the surge of strength on tap in their biceps. As they learn to use it skilfully, their judo ability rises.

This applies to tachiwaza as well, although it takes a longer time to become apparent. It may only be after some months, when they look back to what they were capable of before taking up weight training, that women judoka realise the difference weights can make.

It is important to keep a record of a weight training programme (such as the one shown) so that progression and development can be monitored.

Warning

Many men, including top internationals, have become so involved with weights that they begin to feel that unless they have done a morning in the gym they haven't worked. Judo skills are so complex that they need the bulk of the attention, therefore don't get distracted by weights: they are excellent, but in moderation.

Weight Training Record Card

Used by British Women's Judo Squad
3 times per week (e.g. Mon, Wed, Fri)

Sets	Exercise
Upper Body	Bench press
	Curls
	Upright rowing
	Press behind neck
	The Press
	Crucifix
	Triceps push
	Pull behind neck
Trunk	Bent knee sit-ups
	Incline overhead legs
	Roman chair (or crush)
Lower Body	Squats
	Leg extension
	Leg curls
	Leg press
	Calf raises

THE HIDDEN OPPONENTS

It is possible to be thrown for koka, yuko, waza-ari and ippon by more intangible opponents than the familiar flesh and blood kind standing opposite you on a mat. They may not be wearing a white judogi, nor may they have been trained to block your special moves by a shrewd coach. They may not appear to be as real as that club member with the unpleasant style who negates your upright posture and clean attacks, and always manages to knock you down for a koka just before the randori comes to an end. They may not appear as directly painful as that aggressive and patronising Dan grade who seems to take delight in bruising your ribs so unnecessarily when your skilful groundwork defence has prevented her from getting an outright point.

There are a whole range of obstacles, from the frustrating to the downright dangerous, that are inevitably encountered during a judo career, whether that career is a top international one, or revolves mainly around a refreshing club practice. In short, there are

wk 1		wk 2		wk 3		wk 4		wk 5		wk 6		wk 7		wk 8		wk 9		wk 10		wk 11		wk 12		wk 13	
kg	rep	kg	rep	kg	rep	kg	rep	kg	rep	kg	rep	kg	rep	kg	rep	kg	rep	kg	rep	kg	rep	kg	rep	kg	rep

any number of reasons why we lose in a competition, or why we should tone down the practice, or have a break, or stop altogether and take up golf.

After all, judo is often painful, competitive, complicated, apparently unrefined, sometimes dangerous, and always tiring and sweaty. The technique you have practised so diligently for three or four months shows no sign of working, and the ones you have always relied on stop working for some unaccountable reason. The dojo is boiling hot in the summer and freezing cold in the winter, and if you don't maintain a modicum of fitness – which means running and training in all weathers – the randori becomes exhausting and your skill levels drop.

Your local rival took six months off judo to go out on the town, but came back in time for the county competition and took a split decision off you with seventeen flop and drop *Seoi-nages* without giving you a chance to show your new *Tai-otoshi*. You took part in a team competition, were the last to fight with the championship depending upon that one result, and you blew it.

So why do you do judo?

It is important to have a very clear idea of why you are doing judo and what are your goals, both in the long term and short term. Are you stimulated by the competitive aspect of judo? In that case, to what level do you aspire? Are you aiming for local, county, national or international honours – and is

that aim realistic? Or are you mainly interested in the self-defence aspects of judo or in acquiring judo skills? Is it a more interesting way to keep fit than running?

Having clarified the reasons why you do judo, the easiest method of achieving the objective is to ignore all distracting elements – those which are simply not conducive to the task or purpose in hand. Until, of course, that objective is changed. Human beings, however, are rarely that single-minded. They become overenthusiastic and quickly depressed – often one immediately after the other. They change their minds too easily and too often.

If you are having problems with your judo, or with your attitude to judo, go through the following checklists because the reason will probably be there. These are the pressures, the hidden opponents, that the top players have to contend with, day in and day out; but many of them can apply equally to women doing judo for more recreational purposes. They are not in any particular order, for the hidden opponents do not present themselves in any order, but most women who have been doing judo for a fair amount of time will be familiar with many of them.

PROBLEM AREAS

Training

1. The old favourite techniques are not working any more. To move on to the next level of competition, or even to stay at the current level, I know I must develop new throws, but that needs extra training. Do I really want to do that? Is it worth it?
2. My groundwork is not very good, and if I want to progress it needs special attention. But I hate groundwork. It is boring, tiring, and I am no good at it. Anyway, if I get into trouble on the ground, I can always defend and, at the first opportunity, stand up – can't I?
3. I don't like practising with that person. She is too strong/too defensive/too awkward/too aggressive; I always seem to get injured; there is a clash of styles.
4. I am aching from last night's practice. I worked hard there anyway, so I'll lie in a little this morning. I'll give the run a miss.
5. I don't like running, it is boring. To be fit for judo you should do judo, not running.
6. I hate weight training. It hurts and it is boring. It will slow me down. I can't see my judo getting any better.

Internal Squabbles in the Squad

1. I can't stand Jane. I don't want to train with her. Coach: 'You are all in the squad, so you must learn to get along with each other.'
2. I don't want to train with my rivals in my weight category in the squad. Coach: 'Understandable to some extent, particularly for the top players, but sometimes it is unavoidable.'

Coaches or Instructors

The problems that arise in this area can be numerous, particularly in a sport like judo where a coach generally has to look after not only individuals but also the squad as a whole. What may be good for one person, may not benefit the squad or the country in the long run. Resentment and frustration inevitably occur; and problems players face in other areas can be projected on to the coach. Among the most common problems are:

1. Resentment at not being picked for an event.
2. Frustration because the coach 'didn't understand my problem'.
3. Advice from the national coach contradicts advice from the local coach.

Lack of Facilities

1. Inadequate dojo, inadequate ancillary facilities such as weights or sauna.
2. Lack of suitable training partners, either in terms of weight or equal technical standard.

Friends

1. Some boy-friends are very supportive, but others can resent the fact that most evenings are times for training not entertainment. This pressure can increase with age, from both the man's and the woman's point of view.
2. The unsociable hours limit opportunities to maintain friends outside judo.
3. Therefore, most friends are judo friends, which makes for a rather insular existence.

Parents

1. Parents can be very supportive, but can sometimes come between coach and player.
2. They can be pushy and have expectations that are simply too high, because they do not realise how long it takes to develop new skills in judo.
3. They can be understandably concerned that the hours spent on judo may be better used studying for exams with better career prospects.
4. Parents have legal control over their children until the age of eighteen, so coaches need to learn to work with parents.

Opponents

1. Individuals can have a 'bogey' opponent – someone who is not really in the same class, but who, perhaps through a clash of styles, constantly does well. These need to be acknowledged and studied.
2. Sometimes it is possible to encounter an individual in randori whom you fear, perhaps because they are harsh or make you look a fool. These people must not be avoided, but faced up to at every opportunity.

Lack of Funds or Transport

1. Judo is not an expensive sport but it does cost money to train, especially full time. It is possible to become increasingly resentful of having to live frugally, or at least without money for new clothes or decent holidays, particularly if the player is going through a bad patch in judo. In the end, it is the individual player's choice: to train or not to train and not to complain of the cost.
2. Lack of transport can be a genuine problem – how to get to clubs for a reasonable practice if those clubs are rather inaccessible and money is short.

Injuries

1. There is nothing more frustrating than minor injuries – bruised or broken fingers and toes. But that's judo.
2. One ill-considered movement in a randori or a competition, or an accidental pile-up on a mat, can bring a promising judo career to an end or certainly cause a long lay-off.
3. It can be a good idea for top players to take out a private medical insurance so that they can get treatment quickly.
4. The very real possibility of an absence from judo for some time due to injury highlights the importance of having another area of interest to pursue when injured. It is often possible to work around an injury, but some do hinder any vigorous physical activity.

Employment

1. The ideal form of employment is one where sponsorship involves a full-time job, but generous time off for training sessions.
2. It can be dispiriting to be on state unemployment benefit in order to train full time, particularly over a long period.

Losing and Depression

1. There are a host of reasons for losing, but it is helpful to know why you have lost in order to prevent it occurring again. Here are some reasons, not in any particular order: no knowledge of the rules; self-deception ('I lost because of bad refereeing or a bad draw'); predictability; overawed by the occasion; loss of concentration; lack of mental preparation; injury; poor tactics; slow thought processes; fitness – poor preparation training; overtraining; no coach – self-taught; wrong weight class.
2. It is important to remember that everyone has, at one time or another, lost – often to people whom they should have beaten. That is judo.
3. Mental resilience is the mark of a true champion: the determination to come back and win. When that no longer exists, it is time to retire from competition.

Selection

Sometimes only one person from the club can go to a certain competition. The coach or the selectors decide; it is as simple as that. It is worth remembering, however, that among the criteria upon which the choice is made are: fitness levels; level of competition and standard of likely opponents; preparation work done by individuals; and previous performances.

Media and Press

1. Everyone loves a winner. A winner suddenly becomes the focus of attention, and it can be very flattering. The problem is living up to that attention, and not missing it when the phone stops ringing after a couple of losses: the media is very fickle.
2. One danger is that too much attention can prevent rigid adherence to the training schedule. Losses are then inevitable.

Officials

1. It is easy to blame losses on referees. Everyone wins and loses fights through bad refereeing. Generally, though, the decisions are fair. In the end, the name of the game is ippon.
2. Judo may appear to be an individual sport, but it cannot take place without administrators and officials. They are mainly unpaid and should be acknowledged.
3. Those who are derogatory of or abusive to referees and officials generally gain a reputation for this, which in itself becomes an additional pressure.

Competition

1. In the early days, players should enter as many as they can in order to learn about competitions. Only later should they become selective.
2. It is inevitable that as a player moves up the national and international ladder, she becomes a target. She must learn to cope with this pressure and must recognise that it rarely gets easier, and generally gets worse.

Envy

1. People can be derogatory about others, particularly those who are successful. It is a fact of life.
2. Generally, those who are rude about others feel inferior.

Aggression

1. The simplest view of aggression in judo was expressed by Gunji Koizumi, often regarded as the founder of European judo. He wrote: 'In skill opposed, in spirit united.' However total the commitment in a contest of randori, there should be no room in judo for aggression off the mat.

Diane Bell, 1986 World and European Champion.

6 Tactics

A good tactician can often outmanoeuvre a good technician – this fact alone indicates the importance of tactics in judo. It is possible for a player to have two or three outstanding throwing techniques, or to be unassailable in groundwork, but, confronted by a master tactician, to find that she is utterly frustrated by being unable to unleash them at the right time. The more she finds herself contained by a cunning opponent, the more frustrated she becomes, until in desperation she makes her attack at an inopportune moment. This is just what the tactician is waiting for, and she is now able to pick off the technician at will.

On the whole, women are not as aware of tactics as men, partly because they have not been taught the intricacies of tactics at a high level, and partly, perhaps, because generally they have a greater sense of 'fair play'. Tactics, however, are not simply a question of gamesmanship, a mildly distasteful bending of the rules to gain an advantage (although this may also occur). They are more a question of making the most of your strong points and protecting your weak points. For instance, if you happen to be stronger than your opponent because you have worked at increasing your strength capacity, then there is no reason why you should not use that extra strength. If you are taller, there is no reason why you should not use your greater reach to dominate your opponent; and if you are smaller, why should you not use the techniques that enable you to get under your opponents?

Tactics are used in competition – sometimes unconsciously, sometimes consciously. Despite the fact that randori is supposed to be a training situation, they often appear in a normal club practice or in a squad training session, when rivals may be jockeying for a slight psychological advantage. They can surface between rivals off the mat – in fitness training sessions, for instance, or even on social occasions. One Japanese world champion used to walk out of a room whenever his rival came in, brushing brusquely past him, just to emphasise his dominant attitude. The rival beat him once or twice in competitions, but never in important events; and the rival never became world champion.

It might be felt that this is taking tactics too far, but it underlines another aspect. Every individual makes her decision on how far tactics will be taken, but everyone should know when, how and why tactics are being employed. In order to nullify a tactic, it is necessary to be aware that tactics are being used. In normal life, as in judo, few people can survive as total innocents.

PHYSICAL TACTICS

Tactics can be divided into two main areas, although they tend to blend into one another. One area is physical tactics, where throws and groundwork moves are used in a tactical manner in order to produce the scoring throw or hold. Into this category, for instance, fall basic combinations. A person who is pushed backwards is likely to come forward on to a technique. If tori moves round to her left, it is likely that uke will move to her left in order to remain 'square on'. A groundwork specialist manoeuvres her opponent into the middle of the mat before attempting a throw. A person who does not like groundwork tends to attack on the red line, so that if the throw fails and groundwork ensues she can get out of danger. Another physical tactic often used in top competition is the wearing of tailored jackets, which are just within the rules but which are tight in the arm, so that it is difficult for opponents to obtain a good grip.

MENTAL TACTICS

There are also mental or psychological tactics. These vary from obvious ones such as never showing how tired you are during a contest even if you can hardly stand, to an awareness of an opponent's state. Does an opponent like to move steadily around the mat, and can you unsettle her mentally if you break that rhythm? Does she obviously dislike left-handers, and can you prevent her even starting her techniques by adopting a certain grip? Should you make her angry by aggressive gripping, or lull her into a false security by light gripping?

The training of mental tactics must also be applied to oneself. Victory is not just a question of form. It is generally the case that those who *expect* to win will beat those who *hope* to win. Champions have said that even when they were coming up through the ranks and faced the current champions they expected to win. They did not always win, but each time they got closer and closer, until eventually they took their places on the top of the podia.

It is also worth remembering that the most experienced fighters make mistakes at the most unexpected times. In judo, there is no such thing as a foregone conclusion; everyone makes errors, even world champions. So, when fighting a more experienced opponent, do not regard it as a hopeless task. There may be a clash of styles in your favour, which is always an unpredictable factor in judo. Or it just may be your lucky day, and they may trip over their own feet!

PRE-CONTEST PLANNING

Know your Opponent

It helps immeasurably, in all levels of judo, to know your opponent. If there is someone in the club who always seems to get the better of you, don't just practise and study hard yourself – study her. Why is it that she regularly beats you? If you are caught by one or two techniques each time, is it the technique itself that is really scoring, or are you being set up by some clever gripping or sly combination? You can learn to stop the technique, but then you have to move on to the next stage and work out a way of throwing her. This was exactly the pattern used by Jigoro Kano in the very early days of judo when, faced with a much bigger opponent, he scoured old ju jitsu scrolls and came up with *Kata-guruma*, which, when suitably modified, 'dashed his opponent to the ground'.

In top level competition, knowledge of the opponent can make all the difference between success or failure. It is vital to know whether the opponent is left or right-handed, and what techniques are done from which grips. Which grip does she need for her tokui waza, her favourite technique? How does she defend – by stepping round or by blocking? With this knowledge, it is possible to plan how to out-grip and frustrate the opponent's best attacks and, to a lesser extent, how to make the most of your major throws.

Other questions that must be answered include the fitness of the opponent – is she strong at the beginning but blowing hard by the end, or is her fitness level high? Does she like a particular tempo or speed? Some players prefer a steady advance over the mat, while others like to move fast, constantly changing direction. An awareness of the opponent's preference can be very valuable.

Does your opponent like newaza? Does she tend to go for armlocks, strangles or holds? What are her set moves? Does she look susceptible to certain attacks on the ground?

Is she an attacker or a counterer? Does she storm into the attack, throwing all caution to the winds, or is she a lurker, waiting cautiously for any opportunity the opponent's attack may give her?

With all this information, it is possible to rehearse the contest in your mind before it actually takes place. It is not good to have a set plan, because you can be unsettled if other factors prevent the plan working. But it is good to have a fairly loose plan of campaign, taking into account various possibilities.

An Unknown Opponent

Everyone meets new opponents, and the tendency is to go in quite unaware of possibilities, dangers, opportunities. However, even against absolute strangers, quick tactical judgements can be made from the first exchange of grips.

If the opponent is tall or small, you can automatically expect certain techniques from her, and can use techniques that are more likely to work for you. You should be immediately aware of the opponent's gripping: is it left or right; does she like high collar or middle lapel? If she is much larger than you, she may be more susceptible to backward throws than forward throws. What does her posture make her vulnerable to? Is she a runner (i.e. she likes running around) or is she a static fighter whom you can unsettle by running around?

Does she like groundwork? You can often see this by the way she attacks: if she attacks on the red line only, it is a tacit admission that she is not confident in her newaza; if she attacks in the middle, this might indicate a preference for groundwork.

Does she seem to be predictable in her movements, or jumpy in her reactions to your attacks? This could make her susceptible to combinations.

These are the kind of questions that should be answered in the opening exchanges against a stranger and which should form the basis for attacking plans during the contest. The experienced fighter will go through these points automatically, but the more inexperienced may need to be fairly methodical at the beginning – it may be a good idea to make this checklist in the randori during a visit to a new club.

Your own Strengths and Weaknesses

Finally, in the pre-contest planning, you must know where you stand. If you are weak in newaza you may need to use the red line judiciously, so that if you are caught on the ground you can roll out. The long-term answer is to improve your groundwork, but in the meantime tactics can save you from defeat. Many dojos have tatami with a marked contest area – so use it. Explain to your practice partner that you want to use the line as if it were a contest.

Are your defences against certain attacks undeveloped – do you have problem spots? Do certain kinds of opponents – tall and lanky or short and squat – give you trouble? If so, work out contingency plans against opponents of this kind.

Are you very predictable, with right-hand throws from right-hand grips? Do you have a left-hand throw from a right-hand grip? Do you have some surprise tricks up your sleeve that may work in an emergency, or if they come straight out of the blue?

Are you the kind of person who starts really slowly and needs a warm-up fight before the first fight? If so, organise it with a partner and do it, no matter how psychologically exhausted you may feel during it.

Is your fitness up to scratch? Fitness breeds a confidence of its own. If not, do something about it – well before the competition.

GRIPS

In competitions at the highest level between opponents of equal ability, the contest is often primarily a battle of grips. Through the medium of grips certain things are expressed: domination, both physical and psychological; preferences for certain techniques and basic movement patterns; tactical astuteness, and even likelihood of defence actions. In fact, a contest can be expressed in grips and, to the tutored eye, grip fighting can be as absorbing as full throwing commitment.

Many players will not attack until they have settled their grip. A knowledge of this can be a great advantage, enabling you to attack before their grip has settled, so that they can never get going. It is also possible to create acute passivity problems for the opponent, who does not feel safe in attacking until both hands are comfortably anchored.

Most people need a few seconds with their favoured grip to build up for an attack. So if an opponent does get her favourite grip, then the best time to attack is just as she settles; even if you do not score, you can break your opponent's attack pattern.

Another way of frustrating an opponent's forthcoming attack once she has her grip is to change your stance or your posture. Often, the grip dictates a posture, and your opponent will expect you to take up a certain posture with her grip. If you change your posture, you may effectively frustrate the attack. However, you must be aware of the dangers of different postures and stances against a strong grip.

The basic rule in gripping is that you need to control the space between you and your opponent. The person who controls this space controls the contest. There are numerous ways of doing this; a basic example is one often used to prevent a *Morote-seoi-nage* attack. Both the *Morote* specialist and the defender take a right-hand grip, but the defender moves his sleeve grip inside the arm. This effectively prevents the arm being brought across for *Morote-seoi-nage*.

The *Uchimata* specialist often takes a high collar grip against an opponent because it is a dominating grip that controls the head. The opponent in this case must be able to keep the head relatively free, while controlling the space between her chest and the opponent's shoulder. This can be done by taking opposing grips (left against right) or by securely controlling the elbow of the collar grip arm.

In effect, it is like taking the high ground in battle. Intelligent gripping gives that extra tactical advantage, although it must be incorporated into attacking grips as well.

It must also be remembered that your opponent will probably have done her homework on you. If all your attacks are based on one grip, say a high collar grip, and she manages to control that grip, she will have frustrated your total armament. So it is necessary to have a varied gripping pattern and to have throws that you can do from a number of grips, although you will inevitably favour one or two.

ATTACK OR DEFENCE

In contest and in most randori sessions you are either attacking or defending – or you should be either attacking or defending. There should be no question of stalemate or having a rest. But, of course, this happens all the time, particularly when the fighters begin to tire, or the contest is drawing to an end with one player ahead. That player has settled for the part-score win and is whiling away the time – this is when, in a moment of inattentiveness, she is bowled over. It probably would not have happened had that player made a firm decision whether she was attacking or defending. It is the grey area in between that is often the most dangerous.

Everyone should study ways of being active while actually being on the defensive. This can mean moving around the mat, controlling the opponent's movement with grips, occasionally moving in for an attack, which must appear a strong genuine attack although it is more a defensive movement than anything else. Or it can mean active gripping, breaking grips, a sudden attack with half a grip, then back on to the gripping exchange again.

Pacing a contest is also often overlooked. There is a time to go fast with all-out attacking and a time to go on the defensive. This may be dictated by the way you are feeling, or the way the contest is progressing; or it may be dictated by the way your opponent is feeling. Sometimes you can feel them beginning to wilt and, even though you may be feeling just as tired, if you move into a strong attack mode the opponent will suddenly crumble. Sometimes you will feel instinctively that your opponent hates being moved around fast; in this case, even if this is not normally your pattern of attack, it might be worth trying. If you have just been thrown, or nearly thrown, from a static situation, then you must change the tempo of the contest.

It is difficult to learn this other than by the experience of contest itself, although it is possible to achieve some measure of it by watching it in randori and playing around with the attacking/defending roles. If nothing else, you learn what it feels like to move from attacking to defending. The basic rule is – you should be clearly in one or the other, although, from the referee's point of view, it may not be so clear.

COMBINATIONS

In a sense, combinations are the most basic tactic of all. You are setting up your partner by encouraging her to move into one position with one technique in order to pick her off with something else. This may be in the classic throw to the front attempt followed by throw to the rear; or throw from one side to another; or by dramatically changing the level of attack, from an *Uchimata* to a *Tai-otoshi*, for instance.

The essential quality of a combination can not be seen only in pairs or a group of three attacks in one flurry, it is possible to prepare a combination over the span of a whole contest. By making four or five strong attacks to the front with a range of techniques, from dropping throws to a technique such as *Oguruma*, the opponent becomes accustomed to defending to the front. After thirty seconds or even a minute, she will be expecting another forward throw, and it only takes a feint forward to set her up perfectly for a rear throw.

Combinations are equally important on the ground. Feint for a strangle and go for an armlock; feint for an armlock and go for a hold down. In one groundwork flurry, you may have worked hard and nearly achieved a hold down. Your opponent will be watching for that next time, so pretend to go for the hold down, but look for the armlock.

This gives an idea of the riches of combinations. Not only are the directions infinite, but the time-span can vary from immediate follow-on techniques such as the *Uchimata/Kosoto-gari* 'twitch' to combinations that last the whole five minutes.

DEATH OF A THOUSAND ATTACKS

Sometimes, because of a clash of styles or the equal standard that exists between the two opponents, or because the two opponents know each other well, an ippon result is unlikely. This is the time to work for the Death of a Thousand Attacks. Constant, non-stop attacking, made possible by a high fitness level, can bring good results. It takes courage, because the danger always exists that you will be caught in a small counter and go down on a koka; but often the sheer relentlessness of the attack wears down the defences of the opponent until they just give way.

OTHER TACTICAL CONSIDERATIONS

Nerves and Domination

Everyone suffers from nerves. The champions often suffer from worse nerves than the up and coming fighters, because they feel they have reputations to maintain, while the younger fighters have nothing to lose and everything to gain. Most of the champions, however, learn to live with the nerves and learn the tricks that help to dissipate them.

A bad attack of nerves can weaken the individual so dramatically that it prevents them doing a warm-up before a contest. It is here that the warm-up is essential. Often, by forcing oneself through a routine, the deadening chemicals that nerves produce are distributed through the body more evenly and the nervous tension lessens.

It is generally a good policy in contest to attack first, despite nerves. The player who attacks first has the opportunity to stamp her control on the course of the contest, for her opponent is immediately thrown on the defensive. Moreover, it is surprising how often these first attacks work. The first attack has the additional benefit of often dissipating what nerves remain. The judo brain unfreezes and the natural talent of the player can come into action – before the opponent!

Dominance can come in other ways. It is a much used, but nevertheless worthwhile tactic to run back to the middle after matte has been called, no matter how tired you are. This indicates to your opponent your eagerness to get on with the fight and bring it to its inevitable conclusion – even if you feel the conclusion is anything but inevitable. It also has the effect of making you appear a little more positive in the eyes of the referee.

Fighting Spirit

Prodigious technique and awareness of tactics can be of no avail if you are simply short on fighting spirit. A deep-rooted tenacity to win is the hallmark of all the great champions, but it can, to some extent, be learned. Time and time again you have to tell yourself that you have trained hard, harder than your opponent, and therefore you don't need to rest. You have prepared your tokui waza so that they can turn any opponent you are likely to face. If they cannot, by some unpredictable clash of styles, you still cannot be thrown because your defences are strong. Of course, building this confidence in yourself is helped by actually doing the training in the first place!

Rest

It should not be necessary to rest during a contest if you have been training properly, but you may need to pay attention to your breathing. Breathing is normally stopped during attacks and sometimes during defence as well, and an oxygen debt may accumulate. When matte is called, it is possible to correct that oxygen debt with some deep breathing, although this should be done with caution as hyperventilation would make you an easy target.

It is also possible to correct the oxygen debt while defending, without losing concentration on the defence itself. This lays the ground for another flurry of attack. This is of particular importance towards the end of the fight when both players are tired. It is the player who can think on her feet, even though she is tired, and breath well in order to offer a good defence or a good attack who will generally succeed.

Referees and Rules

Every judo player gains a working knowledge of the rules, but it is surprising how many progress to an advanced level, even to national squad level, without ever having read through the rules. There are areas where they are not clear and simply imitate others, and in the heat of contest can be found wanting.

This applies, for instance, to the rule of working the line. Often, it is only after being penalised in contest and perhaps losing an important fight, that players learn what is regarded as 'stepping out' and what is a legitimate move off the mat; or when it is possible to score with a throw with one player going out of the area, and when that action would bring a penalty.

Reading the rules enables the judo player to see a contest through the eyes of the referees and judges, rather than through their own eyes. They will clarify the passivity ruling, for instance, and give clear indications to the player how judges rule when a player is being passive. In this way, a player can learn to develop ways of appearing to be on the attack when, in fact, she is being passive. This may seem to be gamesmanship of the worst kind, but the rules are there to be used to their full extent and that includes working them to their limits.

Loss

Everyone loses, some more often than others. It is possible to become accustomed to losing, although that doesn't last for very long because people tend to drop out of competition when that happens. Alternatively, the importance of winning and losing lessens, and instead the participation becomes more important. This is, both from the traditional viewpoint – though Jigoro Kano was no loser – and from the current educational viewpoint, a popular and widely accepted concept.

A loss is just another experience, and all the work that may have gone in to preparing for that contest is not wasted, as it is there for another day. That, however, is a fairly comfortable philosophic ethic to consider from the position of an observer and much more difficult from the player's point of view – even mature players.

So the top players, many of whom may train extremely hard, must learn to cope with loss as well as with success. The great advantage women have is that they find it easier to release the tension by crying. Sometimes the tears come shortly after the event and sometimes hours later, but if they don't come at all I get worried. Having seen just how well crying works in releasing tension, I now think that it would be better if men learned to cry.

7 Motivation and Recreation

THE EFFECT OF COMPETITION

During the course of this book, the development of women's judo has been considered through the narrow aperture of competition, and top competition at that. This was intentional, for it is at this somewhat elevated level that the truly significant technical advances are being made, advances that will affect women's side of the sport for at least the next decade, and probably into the next century.

Since the earliest days, women from all countries had their own special classes; but that only amounted to separation. Women would check to see how techniques were done in the men's dojo and then copy them. If they found they couldn't do them in quite the same way, they would, in the end, learn to be content with second best.

Competition, however, and especially the growth of international competition, promoted not separation but emancipation, which is a very different thing. For the first time, women could experiment on their own terms, could develop principles and criteria which were relevant to themselves. This was exciting and stimulating – and evidence suggests that the time of discovery, of real pioneering work, is continuing even now. In a sense, women's judo is only just beginning to mature.

However, although the major technical advances have taken place under the umbrella of competition (as is the case in almost all fields of human activity), competition or training for competition is not the only kind of judo – nor is it necessarily the best kind. On paper it is a fairly immature activity: training and enduring sacrifices for years just to gain a piece of tin on the end of a ribbon or ephemeral kudos can scarcely be described as the most refined of human activities.

This was recognised with unusual clarity by Jigoro Kano. He was on the Japanese Olympic Committee, and although he didn't actually oppose moves to include judo in the Olympics shortly before his death in 1938, he was divided in his own attitude. He could see that inclusion in the Olympic calendar would benefit the world-wide spread of judo enormously, but on the other hand he forsaw that this would raise the importance of competition above all other aspects of judo – including those which he felt to be far more important.

JUDO AS SELF-DEVELOPMENT

In the midst of a world or European championships in the last part of the twentieth century, it is only too easy to forget that Kano called judo 'the gentle way', thus placing it firmly in the Japanese tradition of self-development. Judo, he was saying, was not simply a collection of self-defence techniques or a method of physical fitness. Its purpose was to educate the whole personality, not just to train a fighting machine; and he certainly did not develop his system to produce professional sportsmen and women.

Unfortunately, this area of education became somewhat confused with the special powers of the mystic East, which was ironic as Kano was, in many ways, a modernist. For instance, it was Kano who broke with tradition by refusing to adhere to the custom of maintaining secret teachings on scrolls handed down from teacher to pupil.

Kano saw judo as a benefit not only for the individual but for society as a whole, and he rigorously maintained a strict code of behaviour and etiquette both in and out of the dojo. He sought to develop the whole personality of the judo player by insisting on three different kinds of training in judo: randori, competition and kata. Competition was only one aspect of judo training and, according to Kano, not necessarily the most important.

Randori

Randori exists to develop the technical skills and, perhaps, to strengthen and broaden the personality. Randori teaches not only how and when to do a *Tai-otoshi*, but to have the courage to try it even though we know we are likely to be countered by a much stronger partner. In that sense, it strengthens a basic resolve that can be applied in competition or in outside life.

Randori also teaches a consideration for others. There is a tradition of stronger players helping the weaker ones, rather than only using them for throwing practice or to declare a superiority. Real bullying is rarely seen on judo mats and, when it does happen, other players always become aware of it and put an immediate stop to it.

Competition

Competition also teaches many things. It has been said with some justification that nothing is so unnerving as a judo contest: once you have met and faced some fearsome opponents, few things in life seem so testing. It teaches total commitment, an ability to think clearly during moments of the highest stress, and it provides a handy goal which makes motivation in training relatively easy.

Kata

Kano regarded kata as equally important. Most modern judo players now feel that this was essentially a left-over from the pre-video days. In one sense this is true: katas are the traditional Japanese device for storing judo techniques in a living form. They are a record of major judo techniques and how they were used, although not even Kano intended them to become as ossified as, perhaps, they have.

In *Nage-no-kata*, for instance, Kano acknowledged how judo constantly develops through hard work, inspiration and even competition. The second set, the hip techniques, show one of his own developments, prompted by the competitive randori. His favourite technique was *Ukigoshi* but, the story goes, after a while his students became accustomed to it and learned to step round it. His answer, after much thought and experiment, was *Harai-goshi*, while *Tsuri-komi-goshi* was his answer to resistance to a hip throw.

The Gokyo contains many more throws than those included in *Nage-no-kata*. One of the great criticisms of *Nage-no-kata* is that it contains no technique where uke is thrown directly backwards, despite the importance, even in the early days of judo, of *Osoto-gari*, *Ouchi-gari*, *Kosoto-gari* and *Kouchi-gari*. Surely, if Kano was concerned only to create some kind of living judo dictionary, he would have assiduously put together many katas in order to ensure that none of the techniques were lost. This being the case, perhaps there were other reasons why he felt kata to be as important as randori and competition.

This is also indicated by the surprising variety of katas that he promulgated. *Koshiki-no-kata* must have had very little direct relevance to judo even during the first half of the twentieth century, yet Kano included it in the main corpus of katas to be studied in judo dojos. *Juno-kata* also has its esoteric moments, although *Itsusu-no-kata* is perhaps the most esoteric of them all.

Perhaps behind all the katas lies the purpose of Kano not just to train his students, but to educate them. Judo can be, and often is, a rough and coarse business. Randori can be a hard and relentless practice. Yet it is widely thought that judo offers the possibility of taking on the rougher elements of humanity and, by training them, transforming them into something which can be absorbed by society at large. This, after all, is an image of judo which the public still maintains. There is often, however, the danger that you start off with a thug and end with a trained thug. By just doing randori or competition is there not a danger of merely supplementing a baser instinct, even though it may have a slight veneer of etiquette?

Perhaps in addition to its use as a technical memory-bank, kata also provides a refining influence which is a much needed foil in an environment dominated by the urgency and uncompromising nature of competition. The danger Kano saw was that in becoming just a competitive sport, judo would lose its most important characteristic: that it is a participatory activity. People gain more from doing it, than watching it. This was why women started performing judo in the first place, although there were clearly doubts among the misogynist Japanese of the appropriateness of the involvement of women. If thousands of Japanese women did mainly kata for the first sixty years of judo in Japan, there must be something in it.

RECREATIONAL JUDO

Both men's judo and women's judo in the West indicate quite clearly that competition is not the main motivation for practising judo. In fact, the vast majority of men and women judoka are, strange though it may seem, largely non-competitive, although they may enter the occasional grading. This is widely termed – in perhaps a slightly patronising manner – recreational judo. Its equivalent in athletics is the jogging boom which demonstrates very clearly that participation is more important than competition, yet that such an approach does not preclude remarkably high standards, as the individual races with and against herself.

This is nothing new to women's judo – for much of the twentieth century the only judo available to women was recreational judo. The danger now is that the pendulum will swing the other way and that competition judo or sport judo will dominate so completely that there will appear to be little room in dojos for women interested in other aspects of judo.

There is much to be gained from a recreational or educational approach to judo. Most men and women who have performed judo have experienced its cleansing effect. After a busy and perhaps tense day, a couple of hours spent in a dojo can be immensely rejuvenating. The reason for this is partly the same as jogging: the physical effort literally cleans out the residual tensions of the day, and for a period the individual can concentrate purely on herself and her practice.

The wealth of technique that judo offers is undoubtedly greater than most other sports of its kind. Working to develop a good *Tai-otoshi* can be an intrinsically interesting and absorbing activity. A certain amount of academic study is matched by a considerable amount of self-discovery, as the basic action is adapted slightly to take into account the individual body shape, capability and movement. There is room for endless invention in groundwork that is truly creative; one of the most satisfying times in judo is when a new groundwork move, devised by oneself either in a flash of inspiration or methodically as a response to the attacks of a particular partner, works for the first time. It doesn't have to produce a medal.

The learning state is the most invigorating of human situations. Once the door has been closed on a learning attitude, interest and enjoyment in any activity is limited: sooner or later the pool of water will become stagnant. This is one reason why the positive attitude of youth is more lively than the sometimes static attitude of middle age. This is also part of the reason why it is easier to become a champion than to stay a champion. Champions need to develop at least one new technical skill a year: this is not just to have something new to produce in competition with which to confound their opponents, but also to maintain their own interest, to maintain the suppleness and health of their own mind.

This applies equally to those who practise judo for their own diversion, their own enrichment. Motivation in competition is very clear; motivation in doing judo for one's own personal interest can be just as clear, once the purpose has been defined. In practising two or three evenings a week the short-term purpose may be to work on particular techniques, to keep reasonably fit, to improve some tiny corner of a kata, to have a look at a self-defence technique, or to lose the tensions of a frustrating day by having a good randori. The long-term purpose is nothing short of maintaining a liveliness of mind and body through a serious but refreshing study against a background of insidiously passive entertainments like television, which, without an active counterbalance, ultimately turn the viewer into a zombie.

The recreational player can fall into many categories. There is the retired competitor, still drawn to a dojo by the fascination of judo itself; there is the late starter, for whom judo has proved a revelation; and there are those who enjoy the skills of judo but who find competition and its environment a little raw.

There are, however, many difficulties in practising judo for one's own interest, especially for women. First of all, there are organisational difficulties. The bulk of mat time in a dojo is devoted to randori. Here, the vigour and eagerness of youth can set a pace that is simply not possible for the older or recreational judo player to sustain. Each wants to meet the other on occasions, but not in practice after practice. Youth wants to tilt at experience but at the same time wants to maintain a higher work rate; while experience wants to enjoy meeting again the skill and speed at the fingertips of the competitor in her prime – but not all the time.

Thus, while a total separation will not benefit either the competitive or recreational players, it must be recognised that a different approach is needed. Women, because of the smaller numbers involved, need more skill training time on the mat. For the top competitive players most of this is done during the day, leaving the evening for randori. There is certainly no time for kata.

A club that wants to foster women's judo will need to put aside extra sessions not only to offer the opportunity of skill training, but also to promote the various other aspects of judo, including kata and self-defence. It doesn't hurt, for instance, to put aside a couple of hours a week for free mat time, when women can come on with partners and practise whatever they are working on – although under the guidance of an experienced instructor who can offer help if needed. The mat can be divided into newaza and tachi-waza, and everything from basic uchikomi to kata or randori can be practised. Sessions such as these, where the individual directs her own practice, can be highly stimulating, as familiar techniques are honed and new ideas considered.

Sometimes, however, it is useful not to mix randori and skill training. To come on to the mat for a couple of hours just to study judo can prove so totally absorbing that while real lessons are being learned the time flies past without exhaustion setting in. This shows that even skill training need not be regarded as simply a preparation for randori or contest, but that it is a worthwhile and enjoyable activity in its own right. Certainly, two hours spent in concentrated study in a quiet but purposeful dojo can be a refreshing contrast to its normal frenetic activity.

Above all, it should be remembered that women now have the best opportunity they have ever had to establish a feminine judo tradition drawing on the wide range of human compass that Kano envisaged. It would be limiting if, in reacting to its past, it turned completely to competition and neglected the softer areas that were incorporated right from the beginning. These can broaden the base of women's judo, enrich its sport and competitive aspects, while paying attention to judo as an education as well as a training. Such a multi-faceted approach, perhaps, can form the best platform for the next stage in the development of women's judo – consolidation.

Darlene Anaya of the United States.

8 Self-defence

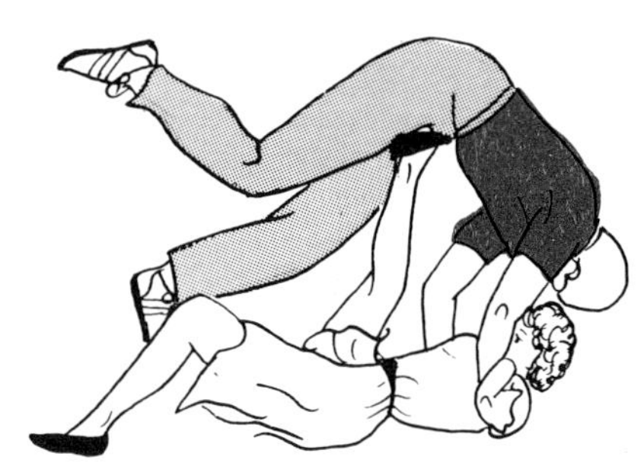

THROWING TECHNIQUES
GROUNDWORK TECHNIQUES

Judo has merged so cleanly with the modern world of sport that it is easy to forget that its roots lie in a highly effective combat system, one that survived both the changes in the society in which it was developed and advances in weaponry. Those ju jitsu roots may appear to be well buried by the second half of the twentieth century, following the influence of sports centres and international championships bringing medals and tidy rules, but this is not the case. Every now and then incidents occur which point to the fact that despite its respectable sport's surface, judo retains its potential as a powerful and effective means of self-defence – one that can certainly prove equally useful to the punching and kicking systems that publicise their self-defence applications more blatantly.

This effectiveness is seen regularly in dojos in many ways, sometimes without the participants even realising it. Occasionally, a player catches her opponent in a perfect throw, so perfect, in fact, that even though she is trained to breakfall and the practice takes place on good quality mats laid on a sprung floor the sheer impact of the fall takes her breath away. Had it happened on anything like a pavement or Tarmac, that person would simply not get up.

Even more dramatic are the strangles. Perhaps because, out of courtesy, most top Dan grades do not make a habit of strangling newcomers into unconsciousness, it can be forgotten that often even relatively small women can put out quite large men as they simply have no idea what is coming and what to defend against. That is in an environment when they know that a strangle is a possibility. How much more of a surprise, then, will the strangle be out in the street, where an assailant thinks he has a weak and frightened woman at his mercy.

The curious fact is that many women start judo because they feel they should learn some rudiments of self-defence, but they continue for very different reasons. Quite soon, those who stay are engrossed in the judo skills for their own sake. By the time they reach Dan grade, most have completely forgotten why they started. If asked by outsiders about self-defence, they will probably suggest that the enquirer learns something else. 'It is just a sport,' most women will say now. They are so accustomed to doing their judo in white suits in a dojo; so accustomed to knowing that it is difficult for them to be really effective against larger men of equal grade in the dojo; so accustomed to having a shower afterwards and emerging back into normal life as if they had been playing hockey, that they forget that they have acquired some exceptional skills. This can apply to many male Dan grades too.

Yet only 70 years or so ago, as E. J. Harrison relates in his *Fighting Spirit of Japan*, many judo techniques were used in the streets of Japan as effective means of self-defence. In fact, shortly before the war judo students were known to do their randori practice and, later in the evening, wander down to the murkier parts of Yokohoma Harbour to search out the rougher sailor element in order to ensure their techniques actually worked.

This was not condoned by Jigoro Kano, who maintained a high level of principle, but he was not averse to teaching his washerwomen certain basic techniques that might help them in time of need. T. P. Leggett tells how Kano saw his servant girls washing clothes one day and instructed them to make the downward movement with a specific and sharp action of the hand, rather than a lax motion. Although he didn't say why they should do this, they obeyed. Some months later, one of the women was accosted while walking home at night. The man grabbed her uncouthly, and she immediately responded with this sharp hand movement, broke his wrist and ran home safely. One of the reasons for the success of the defence was probably that the action was totally spontaneous.

Something similar occurred in a more modern example, which took place in London shortly before this book was written. A 13-year-old girl, who had been doing judo at a local club for some time, was attacked by a mature man. Quite spontaneously, she threw him with a hip or shoulder throw (such was the spontaneity that she can't remember what it was) and, caught totally by surprise, he was lifted into the air and came down sharply on the pavement, dislocating his shoulder. Sensibly, she didn't try to do anything more, but just took to her heels and got home safely.

Such are two examples of judo in action. The last example, predictably, made headlines in all the newspapers, and nowhere was it regarded with more surprise than in judo clubs themselves. Frankly, no 13-year-old girl is going to turn a mature man over and dislocate his shoulder in a judo club, but it can happen out in the street, where good basic judo technique can be supported by the surprise factor.

FANTASY AND FACT

There is a marvellous picture in the Kodokan Illustrated (judo's equivalent to the King James Authorised Version of the Bible) of a delicate woman in a kimono overturning a huge swarthy lout with the slight pressure of one manicured finger. Judo players laugh, but it is remarkable how this image of judo has persisted. Paradoxically, at the same time, its standing as a self-defence system is very low against other systems gathered under the umbrella of the martial arts.

Of course, neither extreme view is true. Common sense dictates that a small woman is unlikely to be able to floor a muscled thug, and certainly not in a kimono. Yet there is that story of the 13-year-old. Most male judo players who have practised with technically proficient women judo players will admit that the women will not only occasionally surprise them, but would prove extremely difficult to catch and assault.

However, judo skills generally take time to develop, certainly to the level where they would be of use in a real situation. Apart from the exceptions that always exist, only women of 1st Dan and above could be said to have acquired sufficient skill to be able to give a good account of themselves in a difficult situation. In this sense, the proponents of other martial art systems may have a point when they look askance at judo as self-defence, although many of the punching and kicking systems also take time to gain proficiency.

Women cannot expect to take an eight-week course in judo and walk out confidently into the urban streets at night under the impression that they will be able to handle any situation. Life is not like that, and neither is judo. Very few judo clubs now teach the little ju jitsu tricks – such as taking the little fingers of the hand that has grabbed you, or simple wrist locks or basic blows – which were fairly common in clubs around the time of the Second World War. In many ways this is a pity, because these are part of judo as

Jigoro Kano envisaged it, and they add to its richness and diversity. In fact, this was one reason why Kano was concerned that judo should not become limited by the needs and rules of competitive sport.

A generation of judo teachers is now emerging who have grown up entirely in a sports environment and who have never been through self-defence courses or learned techniques which, although part of the judo heritage, conflict with modern sports rules and are therefore regarded as irrelevant. Many of them have never done judo wearing ordinary clothes, and this also makes a difference. If judo players were attacked in the street, they would probably give a better account of themselves if they were wearing judogi than if they were wearing ordinary clothes: they are used to fighting in white.

THE VALUE OF JUDO

Despite all this, normal judo practice teaches some fundamental lessons in self-defence which are invaluable and which are not easily duplicated in other formal combat systems. Curiously, despite the problem of the differences in size and strength, there is a sense in which judo is particularly applicable to women. Most men who attack women to rape or mug tend to grab them, not punch them. Male attackers, on the whole, are prepared to come close to a woman because they are not so afraid of a punch or kick in response: they expect women to wilt.

Judo is the perfect training for such a situation. In every practice, women are accustomed to being grabbed – often quite violently – and quickly learn not to freeze, but to keep light on their feet, to keep moving and to look for opportunities. This alone is an immensely valuable lesson. The basic practice of randori offers a degree of realism which is perhaps unmatched by any other formal combat system. With some slight variations, such as occasionally practising in ordinary clothes and with the rules temporarily suspended, this could become an ideal self-defence practice.

The ability to think on one's feet while being attacked is as important a skill as a specific throw. All judo players discover, the first time they enter a competition, how easy it is to freeze when there is just you and your opponent and the result actually matters – unlike in a randori when a judo player, if thrown, can simply get up and start again. How much more likely, then, will a woman freeze if she is suddenly grabbed in the street, even though she may have been taught specific techniques to apply in that situation. So, with a little thought and a little extra work, judo skills could prove very effective against attack in the streets, perhaps even more effective than in the club itself.

MODERN JUDO SKILLS

This self-defence section is entirely based on techniques used in sport dojos throughout the world. It is written with the practising judo player in mind, and assumes no extra knowledge of ju jitsu, special self-defence tricks, or kata such as *Kime-no-Kata* or *Goshin-Jitsu-no-Kata*, although these are often available within the expertise of some of the larger judo clubs and would help a self-defence study. In fact, virtually all the techniques selected appear in the earlier sections of the book.

I have purposely kept the numbers of the self-defence techniques down to an absolute minimum, for in real life it is the simple techniques that work, not the complex combinations needed to confuse a skilled opponent. Against an unskilled opponent on the street basic, direct attacks will fulfill the requirements.

As an overall rule, I would expect that a 1st Dan should be able to use these techniques to defend herself effectively against a fairly straightforward rape or mugging attack by one man – assuming that he is not an experienced streetfighter. If she cannot make any impression whatsoever on the average man, perhaps her judo training needs reviewing. I list some specific ideas for self-defence practice at the end of this section.

First and foremost, however, a woman must know her limitations. It is extremely unlikely that even a capable senior grade will be able to dispose of more than one attacker. This is the stuff that films are made of, but not reality. It is equally unlikely that a woman Dan grade will be able to defend herself adequately against a man with a knife or a gun. In these cases, it is better for a woman to rely on her wits – which, in fact, may be true in all cases. The judo-trained woman will be much better equipped to be able to talk her way out of trouble because she will probably be more relaxed in a confrontation situation than the untrained woman. It is better to avoid a physical solution if possible; you have nothing to prove.

Sensible Precautions

It is senseless to court disaster, so if possible don't be in the wrong place at the wrong time. When in doubt, take a taxi; agree with a friend to go home together; don't take short cuts down narrow, dark streets – take the long but safer way home. Don't get into empty railway carriages. If it looks as if you are about to be left with one or two men in an underground carriage, change carriages. Nothing, probably, would have happened, but it is better to be safe than sorry.

If you are walking to your car at night, have your keys ready and your hands relatively free. Just casually glance around you before you commit yourself to bending over and unlocking the door. This should be a natural reflex at night. If you are sitting in your car and you are approached, ensure that all the doors are locked, then wind the window down a little. It may be that someone is lost and simply wants to ask for directions, but once again, it doesn't hurt to take basic precautions.

If you have no option but to walk through the streets late at night, do so with confidence. Walk purposefully, don't run and don't shuffle. Research has shown that a frightened posture can sometimes stimulate an attack, whereas a confident stride can dissuade an undecided, casual attacker.

An Attack Situation

If you hear footsteps behind you, first of all stay calm. It is probably just someone going in the same direction as you. Without changing your stride pattern, you could start to cross the street. If you find the footsteps are still behind you, you should start considering the options:

1. Is there a main road with traffic and good lights nearby, which you can reach easily?
2. Are you wearing high heels that can be kicked off if the need to run arises?
3. Are you carrying a handbag that may need to be dropped in order to throw the man. Incidentally, a handbag can be useful for jabbing into the nose, but swinging it in order to hit a man over the head will achieve little except to enrage him. If a mugger is just after your handbag, it is best just to give it to him and chalk it up to experience. This may happen, so avoid carrying things of value, sentimental or otherwise, in your handbag.

As the assailant gets closer, calm any sense of panic that may be rising. After all, you are trained in close fighting. The experienced Dan grade will be aware of the fighting distance; a little over arms' length. Turn slightly so that you can glance at the man, and make a quick assessment of both the individual and the situation. He may have an umbrella, bowler hat and briefcase, or a huge haversack on his back, in which case he is unlikely to mean you harm – you just cannot attack someone weighted down with objects like those. He may have genuinely needed to cross the street, or, at the worst, he could be enjoying giving you a fright.

If, however, it looks as if trouble is brewing, don't wait until you feel a hand on your shoulder or until you are grabbed more severely. Smoothly step to one side and change direction, so that you can see what is coming. Keep moving, ignoring the assailant and let him make the approach.

By this time, you must have decided what you are going to do. If he is big but fat, and you are reasonably fit and you think you can outrun him, do so. If he is young and strong, don't try it. This is the time to play the innocent. Don't indicate in any way your judo training but just imagine that this is a contest – with no rules.

Many self-defence tracts advise a quick and sharp blow to a sensitive spot on the face such as just under the nose, or a kick to the testicles. However, even though it doesn't take a very strong blow to stun a man momentarily with a precise punch, most judo women are simply not trained to punch or kick. They will probably miss or break their own wrists.

So, whereas in ju jitsu the basic pattern is to stun with a small punch or kick in order to throw and disable the opponent, I think it is more practical for women just to play the innocent. As I have said, most men in attacking a woman will not punch or kick first, but grab. This is where your training should pay dividends, because you are accustomed to fast and varied gripping in ordinary randori and he is not expecting a trained response.

The principle underlying all these judo defences is: *immobilise and run*. The idea is not to put the attacker out for good, but just to get away. Don't try to be too ambitious. You just want to create a moment's space in order to make your escape. As he reaches for you and grabs, release a piercing scream, turn in and throw.

Try to avoid being caught on the ground, although there may be occasions when this is impossible. Generally, the strength of most men and the limited mobility on the ground hinders effective defences for women, although once again judo women will be accustomed to struggling with men on the ground. There are things that can be done, and I have included techniques in the later section that again are used in the normal course of judo, but they are to be used only in the last resort because they conclude in an armlock or a strangle.

This raises another important aspect of self-defence. The two main attacks women are likely to be faced with are rape and theft. Though both are unpleasant, demeaning and painful, generally more psychological than physical damage is caused.

Each woman has to make the decision whether the attack is truly serious, endangering life or limb, or whether a failed attempt at an armlock, which perhaps just hurts the attacker rather than immobilises him, will escalate the attack.

This is a difficult decision to make. There are times when it may be better to submit to the attack rather than risk more serious damage. There are also times, however, when the woman will feel she must 'go for broke' and cause as much serious damage as she possibly can. When she makes an armlock attempt the idea is to break the arm, not go for a submission. If she puts on a strangle, the idea is to render him unconscious. At least twenty seconds have to elapse after a man has become unconscious before irretrievable damage occurs. So if a woman does put a man under, it doesn't hurt to hold on to the strangle for a short time to ensure that he is not going to recover quickly and catch you up.

In all defences it is necessary to commit yourself totally to the techniques. Half-hearted defences are worse than no defences at all. If you are throwing an attacker, land him as hard as you possibly can. If you are armlocking him, go for the break; if strangling him, put him out properly. This needs repeating, because even in extreme circumstances women are probably more reluctant than men to be totally committed to damaging someone.

TRAINING

As I have said, the techniques that follow will all be familiar to judo women. The circumstances, however, will not, so it is worth occasionally doing extra practice just to ensure that if an attack does happen, all that training in the dojo is not wasted simply because you find that you cannot operate against an opponent when wearing normal clothes, or when an attacker grabs your hair instead of your lapel and sleeve. Here are some ideas to incorporate self-defence into your normal judo.

Practise with a Man

Occasionally, after normal practice, spend fifteen minutes or so just working through the routines with a male aggressor – perhaps chosen from a group of men with whom you generally do not practise. Just ask him to forget about judo and grab you as if he were about to grab a woman on the street. Use a crash mat, so that you can really throw hard.

Ask him to swing the odd punch and kick as well, so that you achieve some familiarity, both with the kind of punch that is likely to be launched, and with the speed at which it comes. Make sure it is a boxing-type punch, not a stylish karate punch. Make sure it is a punch to the head or the stomach – those are the two main targets.

It may sound extremely stupid, but it doesn't hurt occasionally to just punch yourself lightly on the chin, cheek, and over the eyes, just so that you can feel what a punch is like. It is remarkably difficult to punch someone unconscious; what generally happens is that people are stunned by a blow. Karate students are accustomed to being sometimes caught with a blow, and dancing out of range while the head clears or the pain goes. Judo students are less accustomed to blows, and often when they do happen, both partners stop, with one consoling the other. This would not happen in the street.

Practise in Ordinary Clothes

Now and again, do these extra fifteen minutes of training in ordinary street clothes. It is surprising just how much one relies on formal judogi, both physically and psychologically. A man in jeans is much more of a threat than a man in judogi.

Hopefully, a real attack will never come. It is horrifying just how many women do walk around at night genuinely fearful, for year after year, even though attacks never come. It is far better to spend just a little time doing a special practice, even if it just boosts the confidence. At worst, it will provide an interesting variation in normal judo practice, and at best it could save your life.

THROWING TECHNIQUES

Attack **Arm around the neck from behind**
Defence **Ippon-seoi-nage**

Important Points

1. It is not advisable to do *Drop Ippon-seoi-nage*, as pavements bruise knees. In any case, you want to stay on your feet in order to run.
2. You can either do normal *Ippon-seoi-nage*, with the right arm just trapping the opponent's arm, or your right hand can take the cloth.
3. Once the attacker is in the air, you can either just let him go and let gravity do the job for you, or you can take him down to make sure that the landing is heavy.
4. Run.

Attack Arm around thc ncck from behind
Defence Waki-otoshi

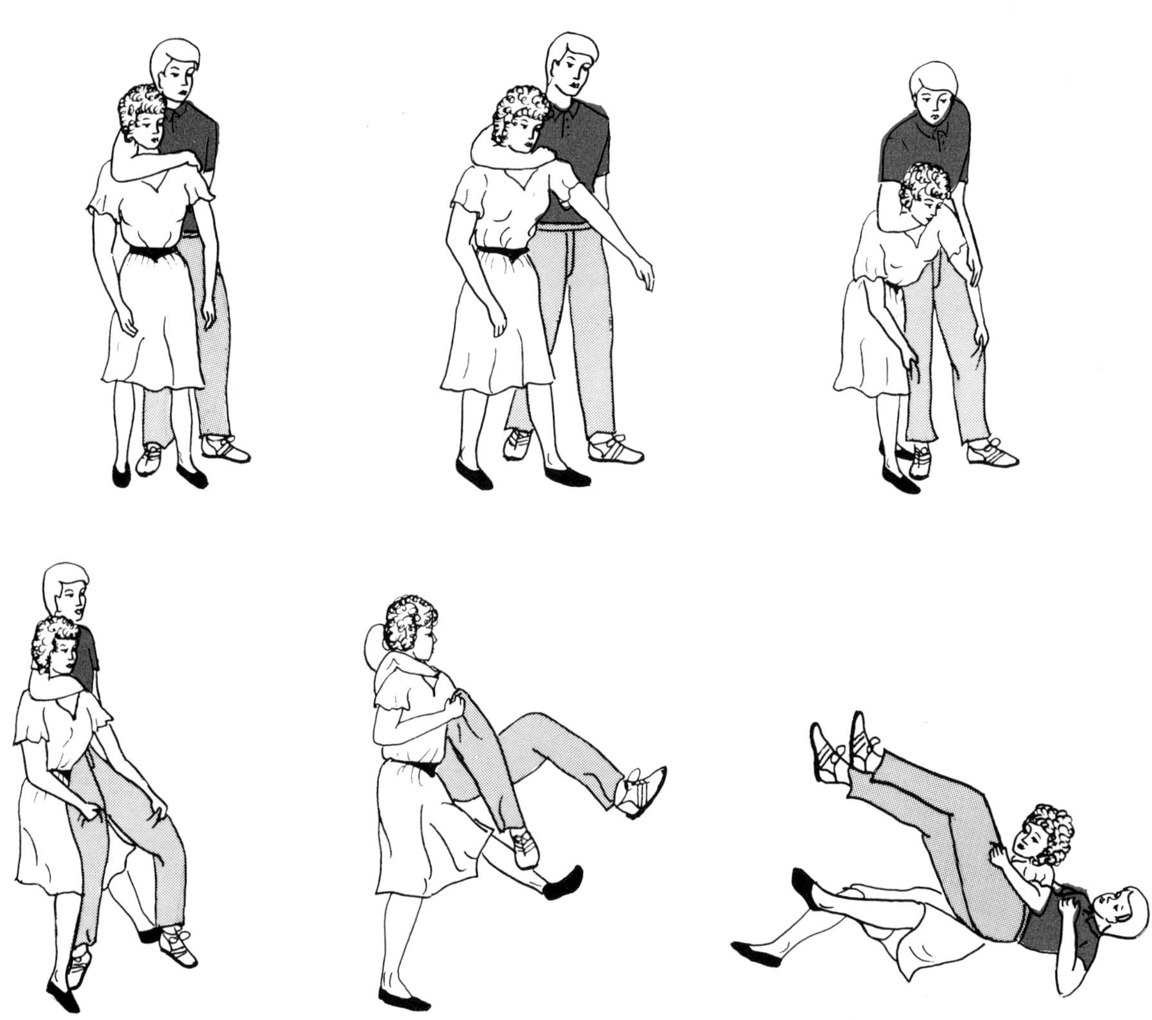

Important Points

1. If he has started to pull you back, take him backwards.
2. As you step to the side, make sure that your hip goes well through behind him.
3. Either just take him back with right arm outstretched, *Juno-kata* style, or pick up the cloth at the knees and whip him over backwards. He should land on the back of his neck or head.
4. This can turn into a sacrifice throw, so be ready to get up and away quickly.

Attack **Front grab, with both hands on your clothes**
Defence **Makikomi**

Important Points

1. Grab either the wrist or the cloth by the wrist, but make sure you have a firm grip before you start putting the arm over.
2. It helps to fall on top of your opponent, as this makes it a very hard fall, especially on a hard surface.
3. Remember, a lot of power can be generated even by a small woman through a strong rotational movement.
4. Get up and run.

Attack **Front strangle**
Defence **Tomoe-nage**

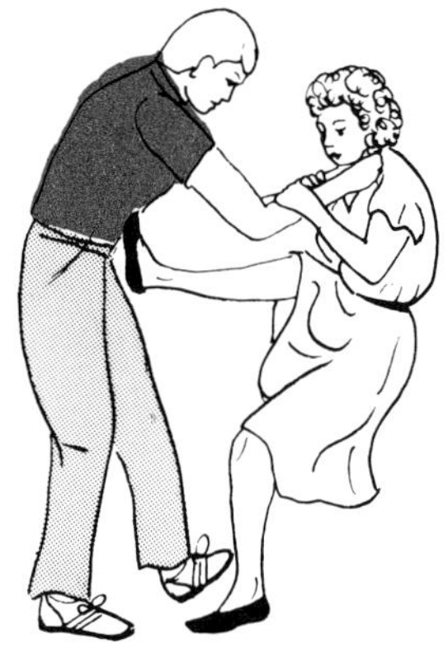

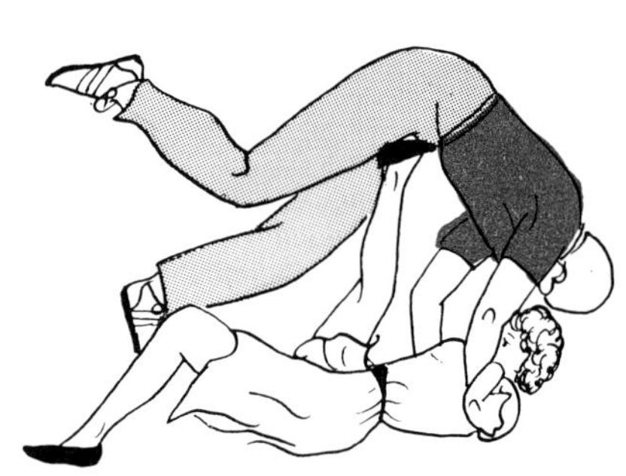

Important Points

1. Grab cloth or wrists.
2. It is the sudden fall of your body weight that launches your opponent to the point of no return.
3. Drop down on the spot you are standing. Don't step backwards.
4. Get up and run.

Attack Hair grab from the front
Defence Morote-gari

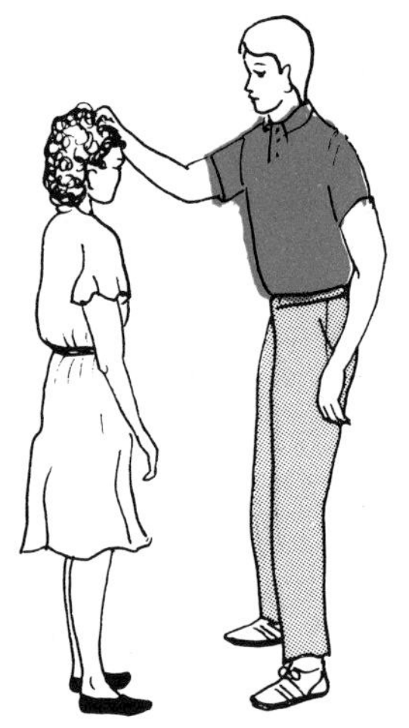

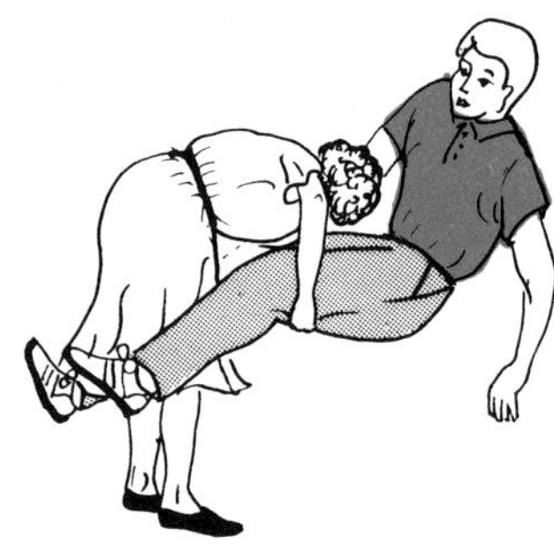

Important Points

1. Don't resist against the hair pull – go with it.
2. Suddenly, bring the head down and take both arms around the knees.
3. Put the head into the body and scoop the legs from beneath the opponent.
4. Run.

Attack Arm around the waist
Defence Ogoshi

Important points

1. Really play the innocent, and do not stiffen. Your arm going around the back should come as a pleasant surprise to him, not as a threat.
2. Only then can you manoeuvre yourself in to position to put your hips across for the throw.
3. Jack him up if necessary with your hips and arms to achieve a clean throw.
4. Land him hard and run.

Attack **Front cuddle**
Defence **Ouchi-gari/Kouchi-gari; Ouchi-gake/Kouchi-gake**

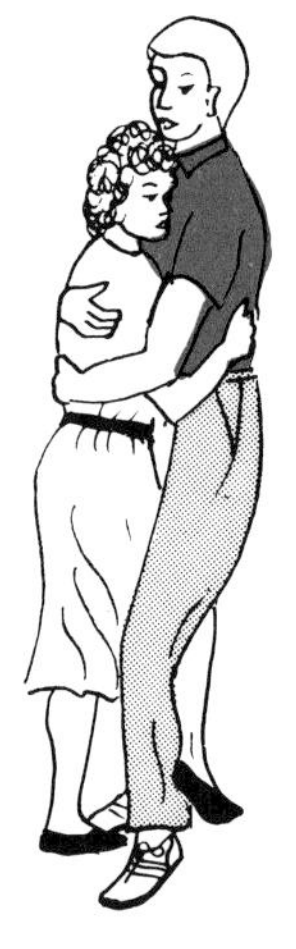

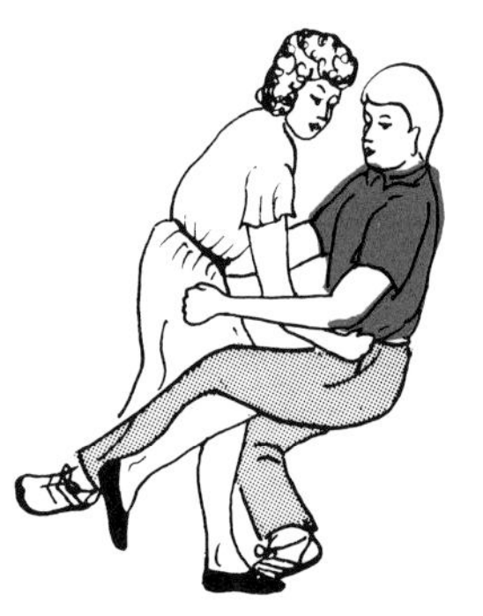

Important Points

1. Cuddle back!
2. Hook one leg and push him backwards.
3. It is possible to knee him in the crutch as the leg moves into hooking position, but practise this movement in the dojo first. You do not want to knee him without being able to complete the throwing movement, because he will still have control of your body and could retaliate more violently.
4. Once he is on the ground, run.

Attack **Front kick**

Defence **Ouchi-gari with leg pick-up**

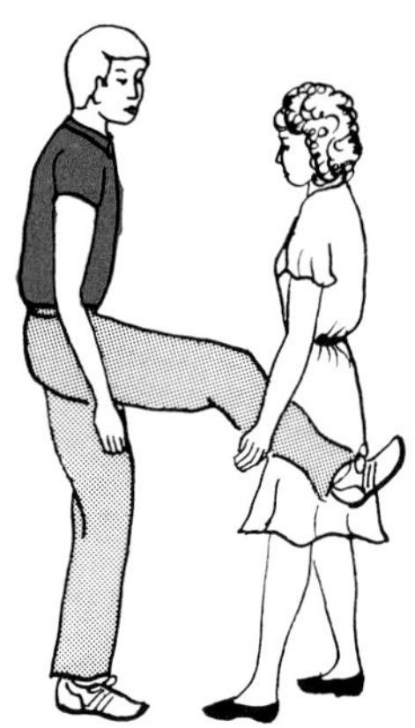

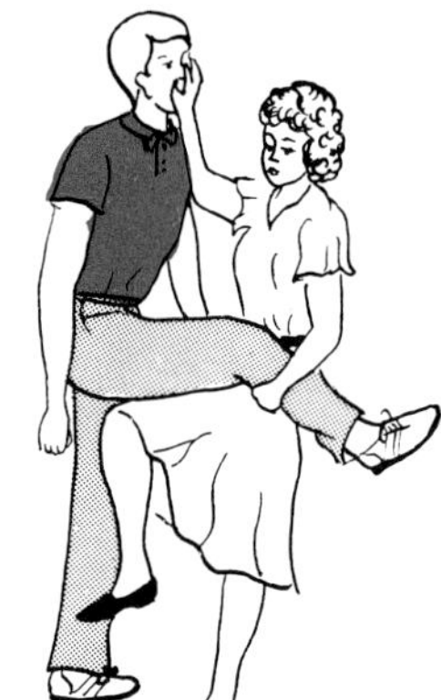

Important Points

1. It is rare for a man to kick a woman when they are both standing up, but it could happen.
2. Step inside the leg, grab it and reap the other leg.
3. It is possible to push against the face instead of holding the cloth. If you practise this, ensure that you give the nose a sharp blow as you do it, in order to make the eyes water.
4. Once he has hit the ground, run.

Attack Punch
Defence Ippon-seoi-nage

Important Points

1. It is uncommon for men to punch women. However, defences against a fast man's punch need a highly trained response, and generally normal judo practice is not good enough. It is worth working a little on basic kata-style defence, except that in training make the punch a quick (although not too quick at the beginning) hook rather than a formal karate blow. Incidentally, very often you can see that a man is sizing up for a punch. Rely on instincts and keep a distance.
2. Try not simply to deflect the punch, but grab the wrist. It is then more difficult for the attacker to hit you again with it, and it is easier for you to come in for *Ippon-seoi-nage*.
3. Although you may grab the wrist, make sure your right arm goes deep into the armpit, so that you get good body contact for the throw.

Attack **One arm grab**
Defence **Waki-gatame**

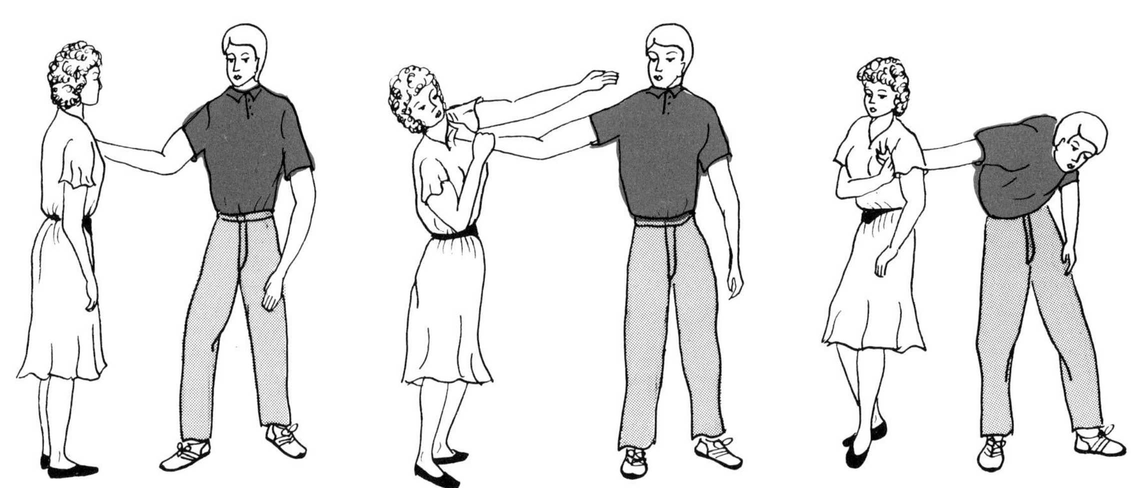

Important Points

1. If you do this, you must be committed to breaking his arm or at least severely damaging the elbow joint.
2. This movement must be smooth and controlled – if there is any looseness a man will be able to use his muscles to pull his arm free. There is no margin for error.
3. The break occurs when you collapse your weight on to the arm. There must be no hesitation.
4. Run.

This photo demonstrates that self-defence techniques are just the same as those used in competition.

GROUNDWORK TECHNIQUES

Attack **You have been caught on the ground and the man is between your legs. He will probably be pushing your upper body down with two straight arms.**

Defence **Ashi-garami**

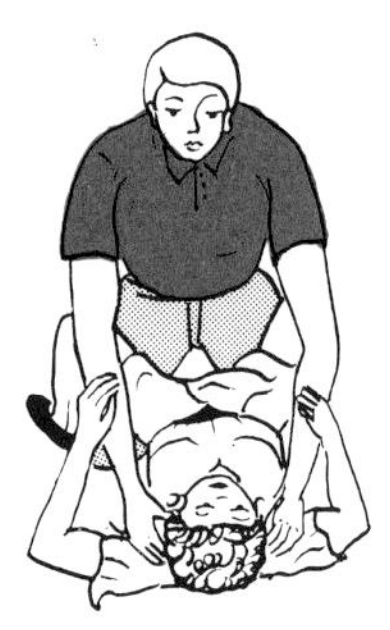

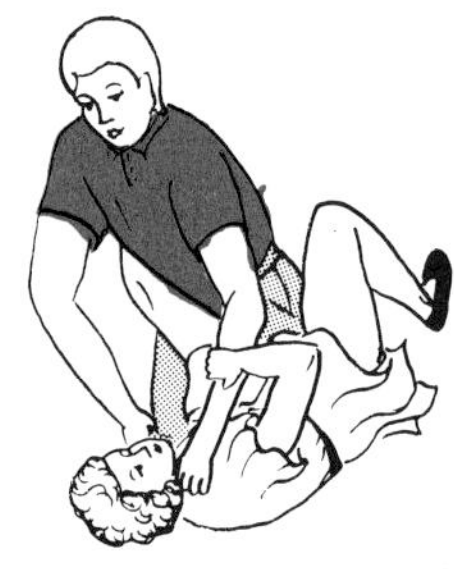

Important Points

1. The object here is to break the arm. There can be no half-way measures.
2. If you are in a tight skirt, make sure it comes up around your hips as you struggle.
3. Grab one wrist of your attacker and, making sure that you keep the arm straight, swing the leg across the face and down on to the elbow joint.
4. Don't be tempted to stop if he starts to shout. This is not a game – break the arm.
5. Run.

Attack You arc on your back and he is on top of you, perhaps between your legs, perhaps to one side.

Defences Shime-waza

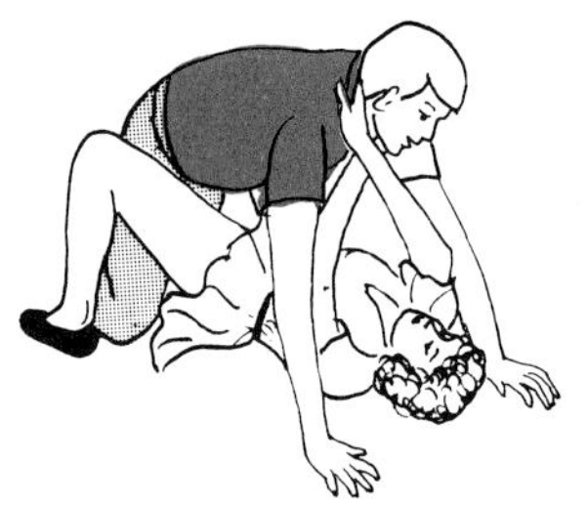

Important Points

1. These strangles must be practised beforehand. You must feel that you are competent at attacking the carotid artery, and have proved it by forcing your male training partners to tap before they become unconscious. It is not good enough to put on chokes. Chokes are painful but take a long time to render someone unconscious, by which time a man will have used his strength to break free.
2. A trained woman can use strangles effectively, because their thin bony forearms can prove surprisingly dangerous when they attack the neck area, especially against a man who doesn't know what is coming.
3. If the attacker is between the legs *Nami-juji-jime*, *Gyaku-juji-jime* or *Kata-juji-jime* are appropriate. The hands need to be deep in and, to repeat, the defender must be very experienced with one of these strangles.
4. If the attacker is coming from the side, the defender can use *Hineri-jime*, a very powerful strangle with which a woman can easily put out a man.
5. Be warned that once the attacker feels the strangle going on, he will endeavour to butt, punch, tear at the face and eyes in order to break it. Just close your eyes (maybe glance occasionally) and hang on.

Appendix World and European Medallists

WORLD CHAMPIONSHIPS

1980 New York, United States

Category		Name	Country
−48 kilos	1	Bridge	Great Britain
	2	De Novellis	Italy
	3	Colignon	France
	3	Lewis	United States
−52 kilos	1	Hrovat	Austria
	2	Yamaguchi	Japan
	3	McCarthy	Great Britain
	3	Doger	France
−56 kilos	1	Winklbauer	Austria
	2	Panza	France
	3	Doyle	Great Britain
	3	Meulemans	Belgium
−61 kilos	1	Staps	Holland
	2	Di Toma	Italy
	3	Rottier	France
	3	Berg	West Germany
−66 kilos	1	Simon	Austria
	2	Netherwood	Great Britain
	3	Penick	United States
	3	Peirre	France
−72 kilos	1	Triadou	France
	2	Classen	West Germany
	3	Van Meggelen	Holland
	3	Malley	Great Britain
+72 kilos	1	De Cal	Italy
	2	Fouillet	France
	3	Keiburg	West Germany
	3	Berghmans	Belgium
Open	1	Berghmans	Belgium
	2	Fouillet	France
	3	Classen	West Germany
	3	Fest	United States

1982 Paris, France

Category		Name	Country
−48 kilos	1	Briggs	Great Britain
	2	Colignon	France
	3	Nakahara	Japan
	3	Bink	Holland
−52 kilos	1	Doyle	Great Britain
	2	Yamaguchi	Japan
	3	Doger	France
	3	Boyd	Australia
−56 kilos	1	Rodriguez	France
	2	Williams	Australia
	3	Hernandez	Venezuela
	3	Bell	Great Britain
−61 kilos	1	Rottier	France
	2	Solheim	Norway
	3	Peeters	Belgium
	3	Ritchel	West Germany
−66 kilos	1	Deydier	France
	2	Kruger	West Germany
	3	Andersen	Norway
	3	Staps	Holland
−72 kilos	1	Classen	West Germany
	2	Berghmans	Belgium
	3	Triadou	France
	3	Posch	Austria
+72 kilos	1	Lupino	France
	2	Castro	United States
	3	Van Unen	Holland
	3	Motta	Italy
Open	1	Berghmans	Belgium
	2	Tateishi	Japan
	3	Triadou	France
	3	Sigmund	West Germany

1984 Vienna, Austria

Category		Name	Country
−48 kilos	1	Briggs	Great Britain
	2	Colignon	France
	3	Reardon	Australia
	3	Anaya	United States
−52 kilos	1	Yamaguchi	Japan
	2	Hrovat	Austria
	3	Boyd	Australia
	3	Majdan	Poland
−56 kilos	1	Burns	United States
	2	Williams	Australia
	3	Winklbauer	Austria
	3	Arnaud	France
−61 kilos	1	Hernandez	Venezuela
	2	Han	Holland
	3	Rottier	France
	3	Hashinohe	Japan
−66 kilos	1	Deydier	France
	2	De Kok	Holland
	3	Netherwood	Great Britain
	3	Kandori	Japan
−72 kilos	1	Berghmans	Belgium
	2	Classen	West Germany
	3	Staps	Holland
	3	Vigneron	France
+72 kilos	1	Motta	Italy
	2	Gao	China
	3	Castro	United States
	3	Van Unen	Holland
Open	1	Berghmans	Belgium
	2	Van Unen	Holland
	3	Lupino	France
	3	Gao	China

1986 Maastricht, Holland

Category		Name	Country
−48 kilos	1	Briggs	Great Britain
	2	Ezaki	Japan
	3	Boffin	France
	3	Zhangyun	China
−52 kilos	1	Brun	France
	2	Yamaguchi	Japan
	3	Sook Ok	South Korea
	3	Rendle	Great Britain
−56 kilos	1	Hughes	Great Britain
	2	Gontoqicz	Poland
	3	Rodriguez	France
	3	Gross	Holland
−61 kilos	1	Bell	Great Britain
	2	Geraud	France
	3	Guy	New Zealand
	3	Fujimoto	Japan
−66 kilos	1	Deydier	France
	2	Karlsson	Sweden
	3	Staps	Holland
	3	Schreiber	West Germany
−72 kilos	1	De Kok	Holland
	2	Berghmans	Belgium
	3	Lin	China
	3	Classens	West Germany
+72 kilos	1	Gao	China
	2	Van Unen	Holland
	3	Santini	Puerto Rico
	3	Paque	France
Open	1	Berghmans	Belgium
	2	Ling Li	China
	3	Meignan	France
	3	Kutz	West Germany

WOMEN'S EUROPEAN CHAMPIONSHIPS

1975 Munich, West Germany

Category		Name	Country
−48 kilos	1	Hrovat	Austria
	2	Campo	Spain
	3	Lecocq	France
	3	Lof	Sweden
−52 kilos	1	Herzog	France
	2	Vasic	Yugoslavia
	3	Matteman	Holland
	3	Winklbauer	Austria
−56 kilos	1	Happ	West Germany
	2	Luzzi	Italy
	3	Reifgraber	Austria
	3	Callu	Belgium
−61 kilos	1	Rottier	France
	2	Mil	Belgium
	3	Vringer	Holland
	3	Nicol	Great Britain
−66 kilos	1	Fouillet	France
	2	Triadou	France
	3	Weiss	West Germany
	3	Di Toma	Italy
−72 kilos	1	Pierre	France
	2	Kuttner	West Germany
	3	Harmon	Great Britain
	3	Cobb	Great Britain
+72 kilos	1	Child	Great Britain
	2	De Cal	Italy
	3	McKenna	Great Britain
	3	Kieburg	West Germany
Open	1	Pierre	France
	2	Fouillet	France
	3	Di Toma	Italy
	3	Kieburg	West Germany

1976 Vienna, Austria

Category		Name	Country
−48 kilos	1	Bridge	Great Britain
	2	Davico	Italy
	3	Hillesheim	West Germany
	3	Tripet	France
−52 kilos	1	Hrovat	Austria
	2	Winklbauer	Austria
	3	Matteman	Holland
	3	Dayez	France
−56 kilos	1	Happ	West Germany
	2	Moyano	Spain
	3	Luzzi	Italy
	3	Trucios	France
−61 kilos	1	Rottier	France
	2	Angelovic	Yugoslavia
	3	Mil	Belgium
	3	Hilger	West Germany
−66 kilos	1	Fouillet	France
	2	Triadou	France
	3	Di Toma	Italy
	3	Czerwinsky	West Germany
−72 kilos	1	Pierre	France
	2	Jirkal	Austria
	3	Salzmann	Switzerland
	3	Jodogne	Belgium
+72 kilos	1	Kieburg	West Germany
	2	Cobb	Great Britain
	3	Parenti	Italy
	3	De Cal	Italy
Open	1	Di Toma	Italy
	2	Thomas	Holland
	3	Pierre	France
	3	Kieburg	West Germany

1977 Arlon, Belgium

Category		Name	Country
−48 kilos	1	Hillesheim	West Germany
	2	Mazaud	France
	3	Bouthemy	France
	3	Homminga	Holland
−52 kilos	1	Hrovat	Austria
	2	Luzzi	Italy
	3	Peeters	Belgium
	3	Fontana	Italy
−56 kilos	1	Happ	West Germany
	2	Ljundberg	Sweden
	3	Van Der Meulen	Holland
	3	Meulemans	Belgium
−61 kilos	1	Berg	West Germany
	2	Thomas	Holland
	3	Hilger	West Germany
	3	Rottier	France
−66 kilos	1	Czerwinsky	West Germany
	2	Mil	Belgium
	3	Suc	France
	3	Droegekamp	West Germany
−72 kilos	1	Pierre	France
	2	Costa	Spain
	3	Gerber	West Germany
	3	Classen	West Germany
+72 kilos	1	Kieburg	West Germany
	2	Schmutzer	Austria
	3	Samery	France
	3	Olsson	Sweden
Open	1	Triadou	France
	2	Schroth	Austria
	3	Pierre	France
	3	Kieburg	West Germany

1978 Cologne, West Germany

Category		Name	Country
−48 kilos	1	Bridge	Great Britain
	2	Vial	France
	3	Jankowski	West Germany
	3	Iglesias	Spain
−52 kilos	1	Hrovat	Austria
	2	Moyano-Luque	Spain
	3	Herzog	France
	3	Nguyen	Switzerland
−56 kilos	1	Winklbauer	Austria
	2	Netherwood	Great Britain
	3	Ricciato	Italy
	3	Ljungberg	Sweden
−61 kilos	1	Berg	West Germany
	2	Rottier	France
	3	Peeters	Belgium
	3	Monti	Italy
−66 kilos	1	Grueger	West Germany
	2	Rothacher	Switzerland
	3	Fouillet	France
	3	Mil	Belgium
−72 kilos	1	Classen	West Germany
	2	Pierre	France
	3	Venmeer	Holland
	3	Malley	Great Britain
+72 kilos	1	Kieburg	West Germany
	2	Schmutzer	Austria
	3	Parenti	Italy
	3	Samery	France
Open	1	Rothacher	Switzerland
	2	Triadou	France
	3	Mil	Belgium
	3	Malley	Great Britain

1979 Kerkrade, Holland

Category		Name	Country
−48 kilos	1	Bouthemy	France
	2	Homminga	Holland
	3	Grimm	West Germany
	3	Napolitano	Italy
−52 kilos	1	Hrovat	Austria
	2	Matteman	Holland
	3	Moyano-Luque	Spain
	3	McCarthy	Great Britain
−56 kilos	1	Winklbauer	Austria
	2	Ricciato	Italy
	3	Ljungberg	Sweden
	3	Trucios	France
−61 kilos	1	Deydier	France
	2	Netherwood	Great Britain
	3	Di Toma	Italy
	3	Berg	West Germany
−66 kilos	1	Mil	Belgium
	2	Bennet	Great Britain
	3	Iglesias	France
	3	Krueger	West Germany
−72 kilos	1	Triadou	France
	2	Salzmann	Switzerland
	3	Classen	West Germany
	3	Litscher	Austria
+72 kilos	1	Kieburg	West Germany
	2	De Cal	Italy
	3	Samery	France
	3	Schmutzer	Austria
Open	1	Classen	West Germany
	2	Pierre	France
	3	Malley	Great Britain
	3	Parenti	Italy

1980 Udine, Italy

Category		Name	Country
−48 kilos	1	Bridge	Great Britain
	2	Napolitano	Italy
	3	Bechepay	France
	3	Hillesheim	West Germany
−52 kilos	1	Montaguti	Italy
	2	McCarthy	Great Britain
	3	Hrovat	Austria
	3	Smilianic	Yugoslavia
−56 kilos	1	Winklbauer	Austria
	2	Beeks	Holland
	3	Nguyen	Switzerland
	3	Doyle	Great Britain
−61 kilos	1	Di Toma	Italy
	2	Deydier	France
	3	Angelovic	Yugoslavia
	3	Peeters	Belgium
−66 kilos	1	Pierre	France
	2	Amerighi	Italy
	3	Mil	Belgium
	3	Mallens	Holland
−72 kilos	1	Triadou	France
	2	Berghmans	Belgium
	3	Classen	West Germany
	3	Malley	Great Britain
+72 kilos	1	De Cal	Italy
	2	Fouillet	France
	3	Kieburg	West Germany
	3	Ford	Great Britain
Open	1	Classen	West Germany
	2	Berghmans	Belgium
	3	Malley	Great Britain
	3	Fouillet	France

1981 Madrid, Spain

Category		Name	Country
−48 kilos	1	Fridrich	West Germany
	2	De Novellis	Italy
	3	Briggs	Great Britain
	3	Nadj	Yugoslavia
−52 kilos	1	Hrovat	Austria
	2	Doyle	Great Britain
	3	Moyano	Spain
	3	Van Weyen	Holland
−56 kilos	1	Winklbauer	Austria
	2	Solbach	West Germany
	3	Beeks	Holland
	3	Zimbaro	Italy
−61 kilos	1	Hughes	Great Britain
	2	Di Toma	Italy
	3	Berg	West Germany
	3	Rottier	France
−66 kilos	1	Mil	Belgium
	2	Schreiber	West Germany
	3	Andersson	Sweden
	3	Simon	Austria
−72 kilos	1	Triadou	France
	2	Classen	West Germany
	3	Berghmans	Belgium
	3	Posch	Austria
+72 kilos	1	De Cal	Italy
	2	Kieburg	West Germany
	3	Vigneron	France
	3	Van Unen	Holland
Open	1	Classen	West Germany
	2	Berghmans	Belgium
	3	Van Unen	Holland
	3	Motta	Italy

1982 Oslo, Norway

Category		Name	Country
−48 kilos	1	Briggs	Great Britain
	2	De Novellis	Italy
	3	Colignon	France
	3	Ronkainen	Finland
−52 kilos	1	Hrovat	Austria
	2	Doyle	Great Britain
	3	Lof	Sweden
	3	Doger	France
−56 kilos	1	Rodriguez	France
	2	Limerick	Sweden
	3	Krasser	Switzerland
	3	Winklbauer	Austria
−61 kilos	1	Reiter	Austria
	2	Han	Holland
	3	Ritschel	West Germany
	3	Rottier	France
−66 kilos	1	Simon	Austria
	2	Netherwood	Great Britain
	3	Kruger	West Germany
	3	Dekarz	France
−72 kilos	1	Triadou	France
	2	Classen	West Germany
	3	Berg	Sweden
	3	Ines	Spain
+72 kilos	1	Unen	Holland
	2	Kieburg	West Germany
	3	Vigneron	France
	3	De Cal	Italy
Open	1	Simon	Austria
	2	Meggelen	Holland
	3	Cortavitarte	Spain
	3	Classen	West Germany

1983 Genoa, Italy

Category		Name	Country
−48 kilos	1	Briggs	Great Britain
	2	Valvano	Italy
	3	Friedrich	West Germany
	3	Boffin	France
−52 kilos	1	Doyle	Great Britain
	2	Doger	France
	3	Hrovat	Austria
	3	Montaguti	Italy
−56 kilos	1	Winklbauer	Austria
	2	Philips	West Germany
	3	Beeks	Holland
	3	Rodriguez	France
−61 kilos	1	Hughes	Great Britain
	2	Ritshel	West Germany
	3	Rottier	France
	3	Reiter	Austria
−66 kilos	1	Di Toma	Italy
	2	Netherwood	Great Britain
	3	Kranzl	Austria
	3	Schreiber	West Germany
−72 kilos	1	Berghmans	Belgium
	2	Vigneron	France
	3	Classen	West Germany
	3	Posch	Austria
+72 kilos	1	Motta	Italy
	2	Lupino	France
	3	Van Unen	Holland
	3	Wantling	Great Britain
Open	1	Berghmans	Belgium
	2	Motta	Italy
	3	Classen	West Germany
	3	Posch	Austria

1984 Pirmasens, West Germany

Category		Name	Country
−48 kilos	1	Briggs	Great Britain
	2	Boffin	France
	3	Friedrich	West Germany
	3	Veguillas Diaz	Spain
−52 kilos	1	Hrovat	Austria
	2	Montaguti	Italy
	3	Moyano	Spain
	3	Heuvelmans	Holland
−56 kilos	1	Bell	Great Britain
	2	Winklbauer	Austria
	3	Rodriguez	France
	3	Phillips	West Germany
−61 kilos	1	Rottier	France
	2	Wahnsiedler	West Germany
	3	Di Toma	Italy
	3	Hughes	Great Britain
−66 kilos	1	Deydier	France
	2	Hartl	Austria
	3	Lieckens	Belgium
	3	De Kok	Holland
−72 kilos	1	Classen	West Germany
	2	Cicot	France
	3	Hayden	Great Britain
	3	Antoine	Belgium
+72 kilos	1	Van Unen	Holland
	2	Lupino	France
	3	Arsenovic	Yugoslavia
	3	Motta	Italy
Open	1	Lupino	France
	2	Motta	Italy
	3	Bradshaw	Great Britain
	3	Kutz	France

1985 Landskrona, Sweden

Category		Name	Country
−48 kilos	1	Colignon	France
	2	Friedrich	West Germany
	3	Briody	Great Britain
	3	Chodakowska	Poland
−52 kilos	1	Doger	France
	2	Kantojarvi	Sweden
	3	Briggs	Great Britain
	3	Hrovat	Austria
−56 kilos	1	Rodriguez	France
	2	Winklbauer	Austria
	3	Bell	Great Britain
	3	Gontowicz	Poland
−61 kilos	1	Olechnowicz	Poland
	2	Ritschel	West Germany
	3	De Brabander	Belgium
	3	Hughes	Great Britain
−66 kilos	1	Deydier	France
	2	Hartl	Austria
	3	Karlsson	Sweden
	3	Bellon	Spain
−72 kilos	1	Berghmans	Belgium
	2	Classen	West Germany
	3	Posch	Austria
	3	Lupino	France
+72	1	Bradshaw	Great Britain
	2	Vainio	Finland
	3	Van Unen	Holland
	3	Motta	Italy
Open	1	Van Unen	Holland
	2	Posch	Austria
	3	Hayden	Great Britain
	3	Maksymow	Poland

1986 Crystal Palace, Great Britain

Category		Name	Country
−48 kilos	1	Briggs	Great Britain
	2	Verguilas	Spain
	3	Vand De Pas	Holland
	3	Biffin	France
−52 kilos	1	Brun	France
	2	Hrovat	Austria
	3	Doyle	Great Britain
	3	Majdan	Poland
−56 kilos	1	Rodriguez	France
	2	Soraci	Italy
	3	Gontowicz	Poland
	3	Hughes	Great Britain
−61 kilos	1	Bell	Great Britain
	2	Debrabendere	Belgium
	3	Geraud	France
	3	Ritschel	West Germany
−66 kilos	1	Deydier	France
	2	Schreiber	West Germany
	3	Fiorentini	Italy
	3	Karlsson	Sweden
−72 kilos	1	De Kok	Holland
	2	Classen	West Germany
	3	Meignan	France
	3	Berghmans	Belgium
+72 kilos	1	Maksymow	Poland
	2	Bradshaw	Great Britain
	3	Paques	France
	3	Sigmund	West Germany
Open	1	De Kok	Holland
	2	Hartl	Austria
	3	Kutz	West Germany
	3	Cicot	France

Glossary

Ago-oshi Pushing; chin.
Aiki A form of self-defence, based on special principles (lit. harmony of spirit).
Aikido The 'way' of Aiki.
Aite Opponent, partner.
Arashi Storm (e.g. *Yama-arashi*; mountain storm).
Ashiwaza Leg or foot technique.
Atama Head.
Ate Strike, hit, punch or kick.
Atemiwaza Striking techniques using hand, elbow, knee, foot etc.
Bo-jutsu Stick or staff fighting.
Bu Martial or military.
Bushi A knight of feudal Japan.
Chui Penalty (equivalent to five points).
Dan Step. A black-belt holder.
De (v. deru) To come out, to advance (e.g. *De-ashi-barai*).
Do (a) Way, path, etc. This word was frequently used in Chinese and Japanese philosophy in the sense of the way of doing an act in the moral and ethical sphere as well as the physical. Kano 'borrowed' it from these sources. (b) Trunk of the body.
Dojo Training hall or room in which judo is practised.
Eri Collar, lapel.
Eri-jime Strangulation by use of collar.
Gake (v. kakeru) To hang, hook, block.
Garami (v. garamu) To entangle, wrap, bend.
Gari To reap, as with a scythe.
Gasshuku Judo students lodging together for training.
Gokyo The forty (original) throws in judo.
Gono-sen-no-kata Forms of counter technique.
Go-shin-jutsu The art of self-protection (in all its forms).
Gyaku Reverse, upside-down.
Ha Wing.
Hadaka Naked.
Hajime Start, referee's call to commence a contest.
Hane Spring (e.g. *Hane-goshi*; spring hip).
Hansoku-make Loss by disqualification (penalty equivalent to ten points).
Hantei Judgement, the referee's call at the end of a drawn contest, requesting the corner judges to indicate who, in their opinion, was the better of the two contestants.
Hara Stomach.
Harai, barai (v. harau) To clear away, sweep.
Harai-goshi Sweeping loin throw.
Harai-tsuri-komi-ashi Sweeping drawing ankle.
Hidari Left side.
Hiji Elbow (e.g. *Hiji-ate*; to hit with the elbow).
Hikki (v. hikku) To pull.
Hikki-waki A draw in contest.
Hiza Knee.
Hiza-guruma Knee wheel.
Hon (a) Basic. (b) Number suffix for counting long cylindrical objects, therefore *Ippon-seoi-nage*; one-arm shoulder throw.
Ippon One point (score value of ten points).
Itsutsu-no-kata Forms of five (the five elements/principles).
Jigotai Defensive posture.
Jikan Time (time out).
Jita-kyoei The principle that individual advancement benefits society as a whole.
Joseki The place in a dojo or hall where the seniors or VIPs sit.
Ju (a) Soft gentle. This word is taken from

Taoist philosophy and embodies the opposite of hard, extreme, unreasonable. Hence the use of 'ju' in judo does not imply soft (as a synonym of easy), but rather reasonable, efficient. Physical action in judo is not meant to be easy (weak) so much as economic. By using the body to its best advantage and exploiting the weaknesses of the opponent, maximum effect can be obtained with maximum efficiency. (b) Ten.
Ju jitsu, ju jutsu, jui jitsu A name covering many forms of close combat in Japan.
Judo An Olympic sport, combat, art, derived from the ancient arts of ju jitsu by the founder Jigoro Kano.
Judogi The clothes worn when practising or competing at judo, comprising jacket, trousers and belt.
Judoka A high-grade judo player, but used in the West as a convenient word to describe anybody who practises judo.
Juji-jime Normal cross strangle.
Ju-no-kata The forms of 'gentleness'.
Kaeshi, gaeshi In judo this means 'counter' (e.g. *Osoto-gaeshi*; major outer counter).
Kaeshiwaza Technique of counter throw.
Kai, kwai Society, club.
Kake The point of the throw, the point of maximum power.
Kame (a) Upper, top. (b) Paper. (c) God(s).
Kani-basami 'Scissors' throw.
Kansetsu A joint (of the body).
Kansetsuwaza A joint technique. (Note: in a judo contest only elbow locks are permitted, but this term can be used to describe a lock on any joint.)
Kao Face.
Karate Literally 'empty-handed'; a system of fighting without weapons, striking the hands, feet, elbows, etc.
Kata (a) Form. A training method used in judo and most martial arts, a drill. (b) One of a pair. (c) Shoulder (e.g. *Kata-guruma*; shoulder wheel).
Kata-guruma Shoulder wheel.
Kata-ha-jime Shoulder wing choke-lock.
Kata-juji-jime Half-cross strangle.
Katame, gatame (v. katemeru) To harden.
Katamewaza Groundwork technique.
Katsu, kappo Methods of resuscitation.
Keiko Practice.
Keikoku Severe penalty (equivalent to seven points).
Kempo A method of fighting founded in Shorinji similar to ju jitsu.
Ken Sword.
Kendo The 'way' of the sword (Japanese two-handed fencing).
Kesa A Buddhist monk's surplice, worn diagonally across the body. Thus there is the technique known as *Kesa-gatame*, but which in free translation into English is referred to as scarf hold.
Ki Psychic energy said to be centred in the *saikatanden*.
Kiai A shout used to harden the body and strengthen the will when maximum effort is required.
Kime (v. kakeru) To decide.
Kime-no-kata Forms of decision, which are the kata of self-protection.
Kiri (v. kiru) To cut, as with a knife.
Ko (a) Small, minor (e.g. *Kouchi-gari*; minor inner reap). (b) Old, ancient.
Kodokan The headquarters of judo in Japan (Tokyo); the founder's dojo.
Koka A score, almost a yuko (score value of three points).
Koshi, goshi Hips (e.g. koshiwaza; hip techniques).
Koshi-guruma Hip wheel.
Koshiki-no-kata The kata of ancient forms with techniques suitable for people in armour.
Kosoto-gake Minor outside hook.
Kosoto-gari Minor outside reap.
Kouchi-gari Minor inner reap.
Kubi Neck.
Kumikata The method of grappling of two contestants.
Kuruka, guruma (a) Wheel (e.g. *Oguruma*; major wheel). (b) Vehicle.
Kuzure (v. kuzureru) To crumble, collapse, break down. Thus a free translation of *Kuzure-kesa-gatame* would be broken scarf

hold. A hold that is not quite the basic or pure form (hon).
Kuzure-kame-shiho-gatame Broken upper four quarters.
Kuzushi The balance broken.
Kyu A judo 'student' grade.
Ma Direct, exact, absolutely (e.g. Ma-sutemiwaza; direct sacrifice throw to the rear).
Machi-dojo Street dojo, small local dojo.
Mae Front.
Makikomi Winding, to wrap or roll up, to throw by rolling oneself so that the opponent is 'locked on' to one's body.
Ma-sutemi-waza Technique whereby the performer (tori) falls straight on to his back to throw.
Mata The thigh.
Matte Refereeing word meaning 'wait'.
Migi Right side.
Mizu Water.
Mon Gate, junior grade.
Morote Both hands (e.g. *Morote-seoi-nage*; two-handed shoulder throw).
Morote-gari Two-handed throw by clasping opponent's legs.
Mune Chest (e.g. *Mune-gatame*; chest hold).
Nage (v. nageru) To throw (e.g. nagewaza; throwing techniques).
Nage-no-kata The forms of throwing, fifteen selected throws executed both left and right to train the participants in body control and appreciation of judo technique.
Name Wave (of water).
Nami In a line, in a row.
Ne (v. neru) To lie down.
Newaza Technique carried out in a lying-down position.
No Belonging to. A link word as in *Nage-no-kata*.
O Big, large, major (e.g. Ouchi-gari; major inner reaping).
Obi Belt.
Ogoshi Major hip technique.
Oguruma Major wheel.
Okuri (v. okuru) To send forward.
Okuri-ashi-barai Sweeping ankle throw.
Okuri-eri-jime Sliding collar strangle.
Osaekomi Holding (e.g. osaekomiwaza; holding techniques); referee's call signalling that a hold is effective.
Oshi (v. osu) To push.
Osoto-gari Major outer reaping.
Osoto-otoshi Major outer drop.
Otoshi (v. otosu) To drop.
Ouchi-gari Major inner reaping.
Ouchimata Major or great inner thigh.
Randori Free practice.
Rei Bow.
Renraku Connection, communication, contact.
Renrakuwaza Combination technique.
Renshu Free practice or exercise.
Renzokuwaza Comprehensive name for techniques linked up in any way.
Ronin An unretained samurai warrior.
Ryote Two hands.
Ryu Method or style. Attached to most of the names of the old ju jitsu systems (e.g. Kito Ryu).
Samurai A knight of feudal Japan (a social class).
Sasae To support, prop (e.g. *Sasae-tsuri-komi-ashi*; propping drawing ankle).
Sei-ryoku-senyo The principle of maximum efficiency in the use of mind and body.
Sensei Teacher, Master (or person of high standing).
Senshu A competitor, champion.
Seoi (v. seou) To carry on the back (translated into English, *Seoi-nage* is more commonly known as 'shoulder throw').
Seoi-otoshi Shoulder drop.
Seppuku The Bushi method of committing suicide. Normally erroneously called hara-kiri.
Shiai Contest.
Shido Note (penalty equivalent to three points).
Shihan Master, past-master.
Shiho Four quarters, four directions.
Shiki Style, ceremony.
Shime, jime (v. shimeru) To tighten,

strangle.
Shimewaza Technique of strangling.
Shizentai Natural (upright) posture.
Sode Sleeve.
Sode-tsuri-komi-goshi Sleeve resisting hip throw.
Sogo-gachi Compound win by ippon made up of a score of waza-ari added to the benefit of a keikoku penalty.
Sono-mama Freeze, do not move (referee's instruction to the two combatants in a contest when he requires them to stay absolutely still).
Sore-made That is all, finish (referee's command terminating the contest).
Soto Outside, outer (e.g. *Osoto-gari*; major outer reap).
Sukui (v. sukuu) To scoop up.
Sumi Corner.
Sutemi (v. suteru) To throw away.
Sutemiwaza Technique whereby the attacker sacrifices his own posture.
Tachi (v. tatsu) To stand.
Tachi-rei Standing bow.
Tachiwaza Technique performed in the standing position.
Tai Body.
Tai-sabaki Body movement.
Tani Valley (e.g. *Tani-otoshi*; valley drop).
Tatami Rice straw mats used in dojos and Japanese houses.
Tate Vertical.
Te Hand (e.g. tewaza; hand techniques).
Tekubi Wrist.
Toketa Hold broken. A command given by the referee to indicate to the timekeeper that the 'count must stop' when a contestant has effectively broken the hold by which he was being secured.
Tokui Favourite, special (e.g. tokui waza; favourite technique).
Tomoe Turning over, twisting over, whirling over. It is difficult to find the exact translation in English, but *Tomoe-nage* freely translated is commonly known in English as stomach throw.
Tori (v. toru) (a) The name used often in technical explanation for the person who applies the technique. (b) To grasp, to hold in the hands.
Tsugi-ashi A manner of walking in which one foot leads at each step and the other never passes it.
Tsukiwaza Poke, stab, thrust or punch technique.
Tsukuri (v. tsukuru) The action of breaking the opponent's balance.
Tsuri To 'fish' up (e.g. *Tsuri-komi*; lift up and pull forward).
Tsuri-komi-goshi Resisting hip throw.
Uchikomi (v. utsukomu) To beat against, go in. A repetitive exercise where the throwing technique is taken to the point of kake.
Uchimata Inner thigh.
Ude Arm.
Ude-garami Arm entanglement.
Ue Above, on top of.
Uke (v. ukeru) To receive. The name often used in technical explanations for the person on whom the technique is applied.
Ukemi The 'breakfall'.
Uki (v. uku) To float, buoyant.
Uki-goshi Floating hip.
Ura Back, rear (e.g. *Uranage*; rear throw).
Ushiro Behind, back of (e.g. *Ushiro-jime*; any strangle from behind).
Utsuri (v. utsuru) To change, to move (e.g. *Utsuri-goshi*; changing hip).
Wakare (v. wakareru) To divide separate (e.g. *Yoko-wakare*; side separation).
Waki Armpit.
Waza Technique.
Waza-ari A score, almost an ippon (score value of seven points).
Waza-ari awesete ippon Ippon achieved by having scored two waza-ari.
Yama Mountain.
Yoko Side (e.g. *Yoko-shiho-gatame*; side four quarters).
Yoko-sutemiwaza Side sacrifice throw.
Yoshi Let's go, let's get on with it. Referee's instruction used after sono-mama to resume the contest.
Yuko A score, almost waza-ari (score value of five points).

Yusei-gachi A win by superiority.
Za-rei Formal kneeling bow or salutation.
Za-zen Kneeling motionless in concentrated thought, meditation.

Zori Toe-grip straw sandals used by judoka when in judogi moving to and from the mat edge.

Index